DATE DUE

JUL 2 1 2005			
		DISCARD	
GAYLORD			PRINTED IN U.S.A.

A WORLD
OF WHEELS

A World of Wheels

Cars of the Fifties

Goodbye Seller's Market

Michael Sedgwick

MASON CREST PUBLISHERS, INC.

A World of Wheels - **Cars of the Fifties**

World copyright © 2002
Nordbok International,
P.O. 7095, SE 402 32 Gothenburg, Sweden

This edition is published in 2002 by Mason Crest Publishers Inc.
370 Reed Road, Broomall, PA 19008, USA
(866) MCP-BOOK (toll free).
www.masoncrest.com

Cover: Bengt Ason Holm

First printing
1 2 3 4 5 6 7 8 9 10
Library of Congress Cataloging-in-Publication Data on file at the Library of Congress

ISBN 1-59084-486-6

Printed & bound in The Hashemite Kingdom of Jordan 2002

CONTENTS

1

SELLER'S MARKET, ADIEU

The important new cars of the 1950–51 season were the Chrysler V-8 in America, the Mk.VII Jaguar and the Ford Consul and Zephyr in Great Britain, the Simca Aronde in France and, from Germany, the first fresh models of Mercedes-Benz since the 1936 Berlin Show. These two years combined would see 2,648,673 Chevrolets, 2,087,892 Fords, and 1,193,129 Plymouths pouring off Detroit's assembly lines—big business beside the 229,800 Fiats, 186,851 Renaults, and 175,974 Volkswagens contributed by western Europe's three leading producers. By contrast, the entire Japanese passenger-car output accounted for 5,205 units, of which precisely six were exported.

Outside America, waiting lists remained the order of the day. On a cheap British family saloon, three years were quoted: for Jaguars, or anything else sporting that appealed to customers in the United States, there was no guarantee of home-market deliveries at all. Germany still had her war losses to make up, and few examples of the sub-utility 2CV Citroën trickled onto France's *routes nationales* although it had been visible since 1948. If petrol rationing belonged to the past, the mania for mobility did not. One tended to set one's sights on any car, however old, rather than dreaming of the latest models on their turntables at Earls Court, the Grand Palais, or the exhibition halls of Turin and Geneva. Even in 1952, the Family Ten class with a capacity around 1.2 litres, for which a Briton had paid £175 ($875) new in 1939, was likely to cost double that sum at the local used-car lot. True, the current dollar equation of $900 sounded less inflationary, but sterling had been devalued twice since the outbreak of war.

Further, one took what one's domestic industry offered. Before the war, and despite the savage protectionism of France, Italy, and Czechoslovakia, a foreign car could be bought in most countries. Yet now, only the creditor nations—and those without any automobile industry—purchased from abroad. The foreigners were shut out of Britain until 1954, and not until the end of our first decade was a French, German, or Italian motorist able to choose among the world's products. The 1965 West German buyers' guide listed nine American, seven British, six Italian, four French, and two Swedish makes, plus one each from Austria, Holland, and Czechoslovakia, whereas in 1951 a citizen of the *Bundesrepublik* faced an effective range of just thirteen models, all German, from nine factories.

Better things were on the way. The 1960s would mark the zenith of the motor car as personal transportation. It advanced technically as well as in sheer numbers, and its progress was unbridled. It grew bigger (especially in America), faster, and more efficient. While the 180 horsepower of a Chrysler V-8, and the 160 hp of a six-cylinder Jaguar, were

exceptional in 1951, they became the expected norm for almost any engine size over 3 litres at the beginning of the 1970s. In addition, there were few rules about safety and pollution. Even in the 1960s, Ralph Nader was a voice crying in the wilderness, and most car-lovers hoped he would stay that way. As late as 1969, one could drive legally without a seat-belt all over the world. Overall speed limits were largely confined to the United States, and so was a vocal anti-motorists' lobby against cars. On the contrary, advertising agencies churned out copy to promote the liberating influences of the automobile. Thus a vicious circle arose—more cars led to more railway closures, so the need for personal transportation increased.

The big problems involved congestion. It bred traffic jams of prodigious length, particularly in countries like Britain, as yet barely launched into the motorway age. The classic urban bottlenecks—Sydney Harbour Bridge, the Golden Gate Bridge in San Francisco, the freeway link between Los Angeles and the San Fernando Valley—became nightmares at every rush-hour. A snarl-up 35 miles (56 km) long was recorded in Devonshire during a British bank-holiday weekend in 1964. Another evil, overdependence on the automobile, took more time to be exposed in full, notably after the energy crisis of 1973. Nobody had anticipated a dearth of cheap oil, although a warning note had already been struck in 1956 when the Egyptians closed the Suez Canal and Arab protests answered Western meddling. Europe then suddenly returned to a 1940s situation and, while the shortage lasted only seven months without any punitive restrictions, it was surprising to find how little one could do on an allocation of sixty litres (fifteen gallons) per month.

With the spread of car ownership—Italy's registrations, a mere 342,000 in 1950, had passed the million mark in the year of Suez—came a more critical attitude toward the car itself. This had not only been stultified by the shortages of the 1940s. A German who bought a new Opel in 1930 was probably disposed to favour the same make twenty-five years later, without too close a look at rival Borgwards, DKWs, Fords, or Volkswagens, all to a certain extent competitive. An Italian's choice still lay between Fiat and abstinence, but France's big three (Citroën, Peugeot, Renault) and Britain's big six (Austin, Nuffield, Rootes, Standard, Ford, Vauxhall) all had their devoted adherents. In America, matters were even worse, with a totally uneducated public overwhelmed by propaganda and advertising jargon, while press road tests in the European sense did not exist before 1950. British and French tests, although rather naive, at least told the customer what kind of car he was buying, on the basis of some performance statistics.

State of the art in America at the end of the forties.

(*Above*) On the 1948 Cadillac, the curved windscreen, wide rear window, and vestigial tail fins (inspired by the wartime Lockheed P-38 twin-engined fighter aircraft) indicate the shape of things to come, and most of that season's cars were equipped with the Hydramatic automatic transmission first seen on 1940 Oldsmobiles. The engine is still, however, the good old iron-head side-valve V-8 of 1936, now in its last season, and giving 150 horsepower from 5.7 litres, or enough to propel this heavy sedan at 95 mph (152 km/h). By 1970s standards, of course, the car was incredibly cheap, at $2,833 (about £1,000), but then earnings were lower, too.

(*Opposite*) Stylewise, the 1950 Oldsmobile Rocket 88 fastback coupé belongs to an older generation, that of 1941, when this body style (first tried out by General Motors' Australian subsidiary, Holden, in 1935) became fashionable in Detroit. Technology at Oldsmobile, however, shared with Cadillac the pioneering of the modern short-stroke overhead-valve V-8 engine, so this car has a nominal 135 horsepower from 5 litres, and a genuine 100 mph (160 km/h) on tap. Again on this one, automatics were very much in the majority.

Now, however, the public started to read such appraisals and even comprehend them. Confronted with a mushrooming choice—Dutch cars for Germans, Australian cars for Britons, and Japanese cars everywhere—they bought selectively. By the end of our period, "oversteer" and "understeer" had become accepted girl-talk, especially as the fair sex grew familiar with such opposites as Renault's Dauphine and the two-stroke Saab.

Economic conditions moderated the boom. In 1951, cars were still something of a luxury outside the U.S.A., along with the raw materials to build them. Steel shortages prevented France and Italy from regaining their full stride until 1953, and the German phoenix was still a long way from its zenith. Indeed, 1951 was the first year in which the *Bundesrepublik* caught up with the Third Reich's best pre-war production, and the million mark in cars would not be passed until the late 1950s. Britain's industry pursued a strong upward path, but could not turn out enough vehicles to feed both the domestic customers and flourishing export markets. Here the "covenant" restrictions, under which new-car buyers agreed not to resell for two years without official permission, were not finally repealed until 1953. Nevertheless, recessions as such did not occur: individual sectors of the business might be hit, even mortally, yet the overall picture was of constant improvement. The Korean War, with its fresh wave of material shortages, was a minor hiccough in the inexorable progress of Detroit. Her top ten makers turned out a paltry 3,750,000 cars in 1952, while the battle was at its height, but a year later the figure had levelled off again at a respectable five-and-a-half million.

The early 1950s constituted a kind of plateau in automotive engineering. True post-war designs had evolved, and were consolidating themselves. The *système* Panhard—engine at the front, gearbox amidships, and drive to the rear wheels—was still firmly in the ascendancy, although renounced by that company in 1946. The other major advocates of front-wheel drive were Citroën in France, and the assorted disciples of the German DKW: its compatriots the Goliath and the Lloyd, and such foreign derivatives as the Russian-sponsored IFAs from Saxony and Sweden's new Saab. Of the rear-engine adherents, both the Volkswagen and Czechoslovakia's Tatra were pre-war designs, leaving only Renault as a fresh recruit. Every full-sized American, British, Italian, and Russian car in series production retained the traditional layout.

Within these parameters, however, the wind of change blew steadily. A transition to mass-produced engines with pushrod-operated overhead valves was almost complete. The vast majority of European makers did favour in-line power units, the principal deviationists being Lancia with a narrow-angle vee, as well as Jowett and the new small Citroën with opposed cylinders. True, in America the old flathead sixes and straight-eights retained some popularity, not to mention Ford's famous V-8, a 1932 debutante. But there were no all-new side-valve models in view, unless we count Ford of Britain's 100E series with 1,172 cc from 1953, which kept the cylinder dimensions and architecture of its forebears in refined form. Weeding out the flatheads took time, yet even in ultra-conservative Britain the bastions were to fall: Hillman in 1957, and Ford in 1961. As to ancillaries, downdraught carburettors and coil ignition had long been established, as had mechanical fuel pumps. Unfortunately, the new high-compression engines designed to run on high-octane fuels would have to await the end of the petrol shortage.

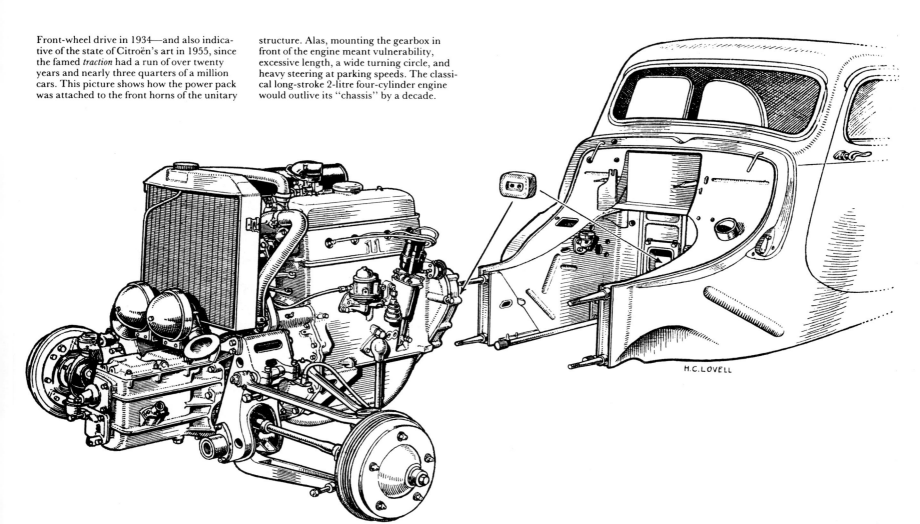

Front-wheel drive in 1934—and also indicative of the state of Citroën's art in 1955, since the famed *traction* had a run of over twenty years and nearly three quarters of a million cars. This picture shows how the power pack was attached to the front horns of the unitary structure. Alas, mounting the gearbox in front of the engine meant vulnerability, excessive length, a wide turning circle, and heavy steering at parking speeds. The classical long-stroke 2-litre four-cylinder engine would outlive its "chassis" by a decade.

H.C.LOVELL

Europe offered no immediate parallel to the class of short-stroke overhead-valve V-8s burgeoning in the U.S.A., where the 1949 lead of Cadillac and Oldsmobile was soon followed by the entire industry, the dying Kaiser empire apart.

The vexed question of the actual number of cylinders stayed unresolved. In the early 1930s, smoothness and flexibility had called for a swing toward multi-cylinderism. This bred not only Britain's pint-sized sixes, but also the Depression-era twelves and sixteens of America. Better sound-damping, painless shifting, and sophisticated suspensions ironed out some of the faults that had encouraged such designs, and by the late 1930s the big four was back in vogue, with 2.4-litre units produced by firms like Riley in Britain, Renault in France, and Stoewer in Germany. Wartime shortages and an urge for simplicity accentuated the trend outside the U.S.A., and cars were generally smaller—apart from that strange phenomenon of the 1940s known as "Vanguarditis", which produced hefty compacts such as the Standard Vanguard, the Russian Pobeda, the Fiat 1400/1900 family, and the Renault Frégate, lasting for much of our period.

These models are often adduced as evidence for the decline of the multi-cylinder engine. Given the continuing spectre of petrol rationing, only just on its way out in 1950, a four is more economical as well as cheaper to make. Thus, a manufacturer rationalizing in the category of 2–2.5 litres will choose a four rather than a six. But it should be remembered that the foreign branches of General Motors (Opel, Vauxhall, and Holden) all built small-capacity sixes: Holden, in fact, made nothing else until the later 1960s. Ford's 1951 British range included a new six, even if their German factory would be content with fours until 1964. Other all-new sixes of the period were the Rover P4 and the Mercedes-Benz 220, although these were up-market items, indicative of a new trend associated with an increasingly affluent society and, of course, with the switch from a seller's to a buyer's market. The customer with £1,100–1,500 ($3,100–4,200) wanted something smoother than a large-capacity four, as several British makers discovered to their cost. They were, after all, up against Mercedes-Benz, Rover, and Jaguar, not to mention a new small V-8 from BMW.

As for America, the swing to the V-8 will be discussed along with technical developments in our era. While fuel remained cheap and plentiful, and automatic transmissions continued to make headway, an American wanted nothing to do with four cylinders in the family sedan, although he might be quite happy with them in his wife's foreign import or his weekend fun-car. Chevrolet's inspired bet on a 2.5-litre overhead-valve four in 1962 came a decade too soon. During the six years of compacts available with this engine—totalling one and a quarter million—around one per cent were actually ordered with it. General Motors, luckily, could afford such a miscalculation, and this "153" unit found a good life in Brazilian Chevrolets. The only other American makers to explore the same type in our period were Willys, who already had a use for it in the Jeep, and Kaiser who bought it from Willys but

10

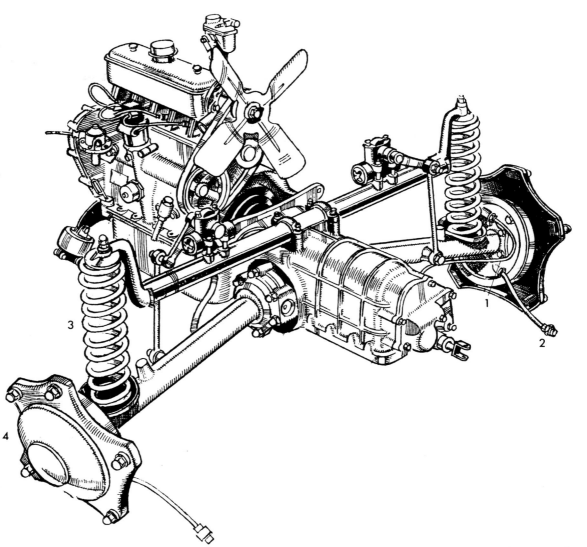

A new recruit to rear-engined principles. In 1946 Renault followed Volkswagen and Tatra by mounting the engine at the back on their new 760-cc 4CV minicar. So small a power unit could be mounted longitudinally without excessive overhang or loss of space; thus the gearbox lived behind. To be seen here are (*1*) the hydraulic foot-brake and (*2*) mechanical handbrake systems, and (*3*) the coil-spring independent rear suspension. An unusual reversion to older practices was shown by (*4*) the use of fixed wheels with demountable rims—but Renault used steel instead of wood, and the object of the exercise was weight-saving and not, as on American cars of the 1920s, making life easier for the ladies in the event of a puncture.

restricted its application to their "Waterloo", the Henry J compact of 1950–54.

Just as fuel technology held back the spread of the new V-8s, it also delayed adoption of the overhead-camshaft engine. The twin-cam units of Salmson and Alfa Romeo had been joined in 1949 by the XK Jaguar, but there were fewer cheap single overhead-cam units in 1950 than in the 1920s and 1930s—the era of the Fiat 509 and British Rhodes, Wolseleys, and Singers. Only Singer remained faithful to the type, until absorbed by Rootes in 1956. What survived was the two-stroke: effectively limited in 1950 to the DKW and its countless progeny (in East Germany, Sweden, Czechoslovakia, and briefly Denmark), this ageless design theme had another twenty years ahead of it, but tougher emission standards would eventually prove fatal. On the whole, though, the two-stroke's appeal was always limited, and its increasing incidence from 1955 onward can be related directly to the spate of bubble-cars and minicars. While we shall encounter them later in the story, they never represented mainstream thinking, and none of them could be compared in impact with the VW, the Mini, or the Toyota Corona family.

More interesting was a pronounced swing toward the short-stroke, high-revving unit. Some of the factors behind this change were already present in the 1930s and 1940s, and can be traced back to Italy's *autostrade* and the German *autobahnen*. High sustained speeds on such roads encouraged not only superior aerodynamic shapes, but also en-

gines and gearing capable of equating maximum and cruising speeds. To see the results in practice, one may compare Continental and British cars of the late 1940s. In the 1,100-cc class, we find the VW (with an oversquare ratio of bore to stroke, at 77×64 mm) and the Fiat 1100 (nearly square, at 68×75 mm), both current in 1939 although the Beetle's engine was slightly smaller. Peugeot, with an eye on Europe as a whole, were moving toward the new idiom with their 202 engine (at 68×78 mm). But more typical of the old guard was Renault's Juvaquatre, an Opel copy with the most un-Opel-like dimensions of 58×95 mm. In Britain, the popular Hillman Minx had a bore of 63 mm and a stroke of 95 mm. The abolition of the archaic British taxation formula, based on the number and bore of the cylinders alone, was taking effect. After 1946, the Minx no longer had to be a "10 hp", so its bore was opened out to 65 mm in 1950—yet it remained a statement of the old way of thinking until 1954, when the unit was redesigned from scratch with a square ratio at 76×76 mm.

Fiscal restrictions on engine size were becoming fewer. In France and Italy, they were still punitive but, as taxation was based upon overall capacity, the short-stroke unit suffered no special penalty. Only in Japan was industry stifled right through our first decade. Misfortunes there, indeed, were supremely irrelevant to the rest of the motoring world, even in 1959 when a row developed between Renault and Hino because the latter failed to pay royalties on licence-built 4CV cars. The French government's view is a sobering commentary on Western indif-

ference: how cruel "to pick on this poor little country which has such a task to feed hundreds and millions of inhabitants"!

In regard to transmissions, single-plate clutches and synchromesh were generally used. Few makers, however, offered a synchronized bottom gear in 1950, one of the rare exceptions being Standard. Even the Americans would not bother with this until the mid-1960s, since the lowest ratio was seldom employed, and more and more customers were specifying automatic shift. The main legacy of the 1940s was column shift, an American innovation from 1938, and bearable only where three forward speeds sufficed. Its sole advantage was an unobstructed front-compartment floor, which made sense in an era when the American-type family sedan still appealed as a "world car". Alas, what Americans term "four on the tree" led to cumbersome shift patterns, the principal dishonours falling to Austin, Mercedes-Benz, and Peugeot.

Nor did synchromesh have things all its own way. Preselectors were declining, and the star of automatic transmission was in the ascendant. Already in 1951 it was difficult, if not impossible, to buy an American luxury model with conventional stick shift. In the middle-class sector, 80 % of all new Packards, 78 % of all Buicks, and 70 % of all Hudsons were self-shifters. Buick turned out two million automatic gearboxes between 1948 and 1954, while Chevrolet, who adopted the system in 1950, were fitting Powerglide to 20 % of their production within a year, raising the proportion to about 60 % by 1957.

Automatics had yet to reach Europe: tooling costs were undoubtedly the chief obstacle, and the inherent power losses of self-shifting would have been disastrous at a time when 45–50 horsepower were the norm

(*Opposite, top*) DKW revival in Czechoslovakia, 1946, though the Aero Minor name is misleading. The car was based on Jawa's licence-built DKW, and not on the pre-war Aero, also a two-stroke twin with front-wheel drive! Beneath the teardrop shape in the Hanomag/Volvo idiom is the usual 615-cc transverse-twin engine. But the four-speed transmission with its overdrive top, the forked backbone frame, all-independent springing, and the radiator behind the power unit differentiated it from the old F8 theme still being manufactured in East Germany. The Aero Minor was current until 1952.

(*Opposite, bottom*) Being up-to-date in 1939 meant that one could pursue themes unchanged into the mid-1950s, as in the case of General Motors' German offering, the Opel Olympia, here seen in 1951 guise with the same oversquare 1.5-litre overhead-valve four-cylinder engine, unitary structure, and three-speed transmission which it had used pre-war. Styling changes, likewise, are limited to a frontal facelift, even the old and ugly headlamp nacelles in the hood sides being retained. European buyers could have their small GM car in British or German form. Neither Opel's coil-spring front end nor Vauxhall's torsion bars made for good handling, and whether you bought British or German depended on whether you preferred four doors to two on a sedan (Opel didn't offer the former configuration) or if you wanted a station wagon, in which case Vauxhall had nothing for you. A re-emergent Germany was already coming out on top: that year's deliveries of Opel Olympias alone ran to 40,154 cars, more than Vauxhall's total production of fours and sixes. The British Bedford truck range, however, sold better than Opel's Blitz family.

(*Top right*) Soldiering on (with time out for a war) from 1934 to 1957 was the front-wheel-drive 11CV Citroën. The definitive 1,911-cc overhead-valve four-cylinder engine had arrived within eight months of the car's introduction. But apart from rack-and-pinion steering (1936) and an extended rear boot (1952), very little was changed otherwise. The short-wheelbase 11 Légère was the classic model. Here, for variety, is the 11 Normale, a full six-seater on a longer wheelbase of 122 in (3.1 m). This car dates from 1951 and is one of the last small-boot types. The light grey finish does not indicate a British model: although French-made cars were invariably black in the early post-war years, the Swedish importers also applied a little colour.

(*Bottom right*) Most modern-looking of the Vanguard-era sedans, here is Renault's 2-litre four-cylinder Frégate in 1954–56 guise. The ideas are scaled-down American, while the thick windscreen pillars and limited rear vision reflect Detroit's thinking of the 1940s. The independent rear springing and four-speed transmission are, however, strictly European, though nobody much cared for the Frégate's all-indirect ratios (this from the pioneer of direct drives!) or their sound effects. In any case, the Régie Renault had strong domestic competition in the big-car class: if Simca's Ford-derived Vedette never amounted to much, Citroën's *traction* was eighteen years old when the Renault made its *début*, and from 1956 there was the *avant-garde* Déesse as well.

for a 1.5-litre engine. This penalty remained formidable for many years, as anyone will testify who has driven a Hillman or Singer with Borg-Warner transmission from the early 1960s. It is, therefore, hardly surprising to find that the only European automatics on offer in 1950 were the truly gearless Invicta—whose makers were in the process of going bankrupt—and the Borgward, which was made in very small numbers and was soon discarded on grounds of fragility.

For transmitting power to the rear, one might expect an open propeller shaft, although torque tubes still had their adherents. A spiral-bevel back axle was the type in general use, and had been since the early 1920s. The underslung hypoid type, however, became more and more popular as it lowered the driveline and, thus, the centre of gravity. The worm drives of Peugeot and Daimler were notable exceptions, the latter company remaining loyal to this configuration on all conventional designs until 1968.

Suspensions at the front of the car were invariably independent, apart from odd archaisms such as the small British and German Fords—and these, too, were in the process of making the change, Dagenham's Consul and Zephyr appearing at the 1950 shows, and Cologne's Taunus a year later. The sports cars followed suit: the MG Midget had acquired coils on the TD series early in 1950. While coil layouts of the short-and-long-arm configuration predominated, Morris, Volkswagen, and Citroën were among those who preferred torsion bars, and a transverse-leaf arrangement was favoured by the Rootes Group on some of their older designs. Ford of France were as yet the sole adherents of the McPherson strut system, which became popular only in the 1970s.

Independent rear ends were scarcer, being considered too complex and expensive to build by the majority of makers, although many a

German factory had espoused them before the war and, on subsequent models, the system was retained by Borgward, VW, and Mercedes-Benz, as well as by Skoda and Tatra in Czechoslovakia. So far, the most important new recruit had been Renault, on the little rear-engined 4CV. But Fiat would leave the idea alone until 1952, and Britain, for all her important early contributions (Alvis, Atalanta, and the latest 2.6-litre Lagonda), would not apply it to a popular car until 1959. In America, of course, the safe way was the known way, and independent rear springing was not obviously associated with painless motoring.

In the braking department, a hydraulic system working in drums on all four wheels was almost mandatory, as was an emergency hand-operated system working only on the rear wheels. The main exception to the first rule was the British hydromechanical layout, a compromise favoured by Rolls-Royce for safety, and by others on grounds of economy. Nothing better was really needed: roads had suffered from the ravages of war, tyre technology was at a fairly primitive stage, and cruising speeds of 60–65 mph (100–110 km/h) were normal for "fast" cars. Your small family sedan could reach 70 mph (112 km/h) but cruised around 50 mph (85 km/h). Handbrake variations were more limited, and the same principle applied to foot-operated emergency brakes preferred in America by Buick and Oldsmobile. The only major heresy was the obstinate adherence of Fiat and Chrysler—who made quite a lot of cars—to the transmission brake, a device of undoubted efficiency, but hard on drivelines unless used strictly for parking.

On its way up, of course, was unitary construction. From having just a few pre-war advocates, it now became the general practice for mass-produced European sedans, the chief exceptions being Standard's Vanguard and the tubular backbone frame of the VW. The method's economics were, in fact, to govern the development of the motor car for

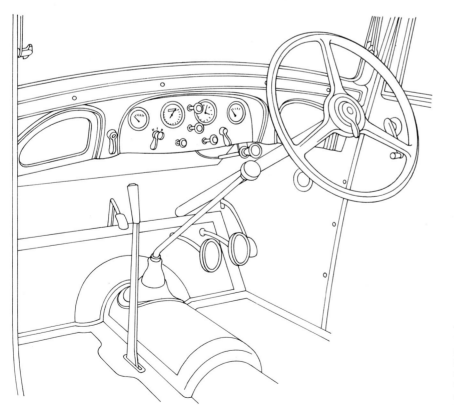

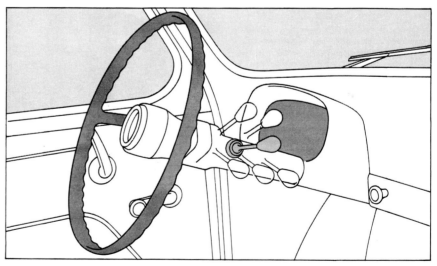

The changing face of gear-shifting: Fiats of 1934 (*left*) and 1956 (*above*). The older car's central lever with its neighbouring, locomotive-sized handbrake obstructed the front compartment, while the former's long and willowy configuration did not make for quick, positive shifts, whatever the sentimentalists said. By contrast, the later 1100-103's column selector took up less room, but the nature of this diagram from a contemporary instruction manual suggests that the general public did not find it easy to regard the new layout as "just an ordinary shift laid on its side". As the linkage had to travel all the way down to the column and then under the floor to the gearbox, actual shifts were even woollier, though the Fiat's was one of the better specimens of a depressing period.

Automatic transmissions. In this diagram of Buick's original two-speed Dynaflow (1948) are shown (*1*) the primary pump bolted to the engine crankshaft (*2*), turning at engine speed. The turbine (*3*), directly opposed to it, is splined onto the gearbox input shaft, and in direct drive it runs continuously at propeller-shaft speed. The other three elements, a secondary pump (*4*) and two stators (*5*), are individually mounted on an over-running clutch mechanism (*6*). They are thus enabled to turn freely or be held in fixed positions. On a two-speed automatic, the steering-column-mounted selector is a simple, if not a foolproof, affair. From left to right, its positions read Park-Neutral-Drive-Low-Reverse. The absence of a positive stop between forward and backward movement was something that would not be tolerated in the safety-conscious climate of the later 1960s.

the next twenty years, since it was cost-effective only in relation to long production runs, and was susceptible neither to a wide range of bodies nor to great changes in style. As it caught on, new designs with a separate chassis grew rare: hence the "Look, It's Got a Chassis" publicity campaign behind the Triumph Herald in 1959.

As yet, inherent corrosion problems of unitaries had barely emerged. Anyone shopping for a pre-war Opel or Citroën *traction* model was well advised to investigate closely—but if it was not actually sagging in the middle, it at least represented transportation. In any case, the only countries with annual inspection laws in 1951 were the U.S.A. and New Zealand. Unitary construction made little headway in America, where the annual production run could be relied upon to pay the tooling bill for a separate chassis. With the latter, too, the effects of falling sales were less catastrophic. Hudson had a bad time trying to sell their unitary Stepdown, a 1948 debutante, once the shape went out of fashion. The sales graph was eloquent enough: a peak of 140,000 cars for the first three seasons, falling to 93,000 in 1951 and to a dismal 32,287 in 1954, the company's last year of financial independence. Nash, admittedly, fared rather better, and unitaries would reach the big battalions in due course, but it was a hazardous policy.

Concerning bodies, we were still in the era of the seller's market, when customers could not afford to argue about style, colour, or equipment. Early post-war VWs came out in a nondescript grey, and most British family sedans were black, Ford offering no home-market alternative in 1946. Even in 1951, Citroën *tractions* from the Quai de Javel factory were all black: if you wanted maroon or green, you opted for right-hand drive from the British assembly plant at Slough. Moreover, sedans were the only style available in 1950 for Peugeots, Opel Olympias, and Fiat 1100s, while the spread of unitary construction tended to

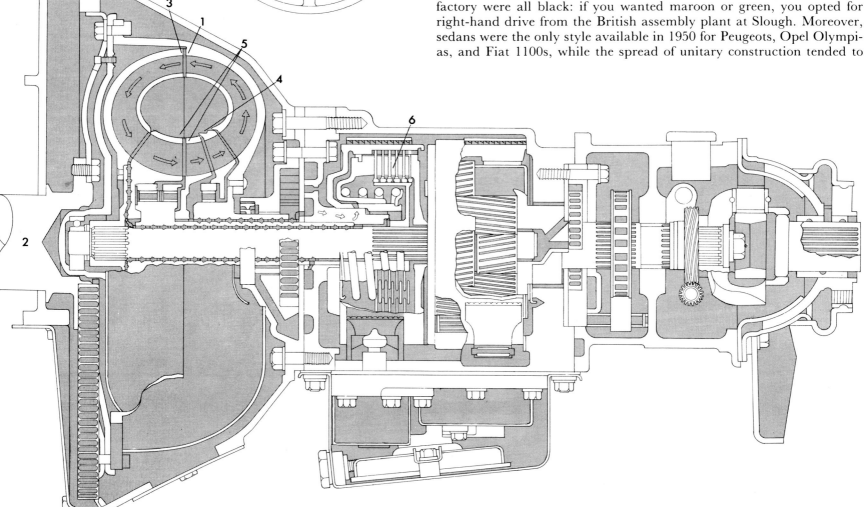

(*Opposite*) Traditional but still modern. It looks Italian, its ancestry is German, and it bears the hallowed British name of Frazer Nash. This is the actual Targa Florio Gran Sport roadster exhibited at the London Show in October, 1952, and a direct descendant of the 328 BMW (1936), probably the best all-round sports car of its decade. The triple-carburettor pushrod 2-litre six-cylinder

engine develops 125 horsepower, and the suspension—by an independent transverse-leaf arrangement at the front and by torsion bars at the rear—is pure BMW. The name has a meaning, too: a Frazer Nash was the only British car ever to win the Targa Florio Race in Sicily, in 1951. Top speed is about 120 mph (192 km/h), but production was very limited—probably less than 20 cars

built to this specification between 1952 and 1955.

(*Below*) The first modern GT, a Lancia Aurelia coupé in 1953 form. The racing numbers and lack of trim indicate a competition version and, like all Lancias of those days, it's still right-hand-drive. But the formula is

the classic one: compact, narrow-angle 2.5-litre V-6 engine, four-speed synchromesh transaxle, and inboard rear brakes. Even in standard tune, 105 mph (168 km/h) present no problems, and one can settle down on one's favourite *autostrada* at 90–95 mph (145–155 km/h). But despite an eight-year run and countless rally successes, barely 5,000 of these cars found buyers.

(*Below*) British chassis of 1946, not quite classical. The Triumph 1800 uses an overhead-valve 1.8-litre four-cylinder engine. It looks old-fashioned mainly thanks to its traditionally shaped radiator, but observe (*1*) the transverse-leaf independent front suspension, (*2*) hydraulic brakes, (*3*) column-mounted gear lever, and (*4*) tubular chassis frame, this being adopted because steel tube was freely available in the austere economic climate of early post-war Britain. Technical progress does not always stem from truly technical motives. One might have contrasted a classical chassis of the same date as on the Lea-Francis Fourteen, which retained semi-elliptic springs at each end and mechanical brakes, as well as a centrally mounted selector for its four-speed synchromesh gearbox: the only feature that stamped it as post- rather than pre-war was the use of disc instead of wire wheels, the latter being normal then for a luxury sedan of mildly sporting character with the same engine capacity.

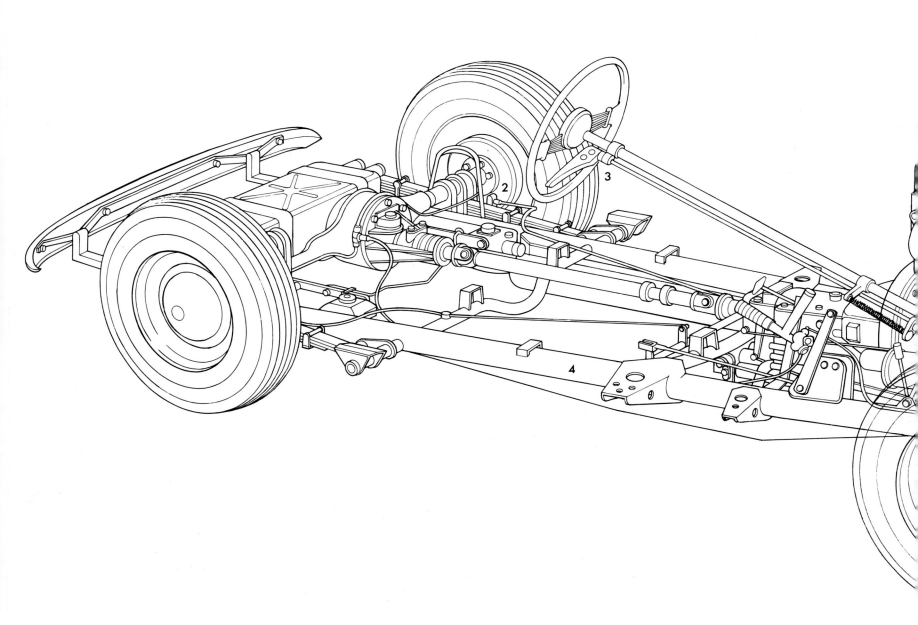

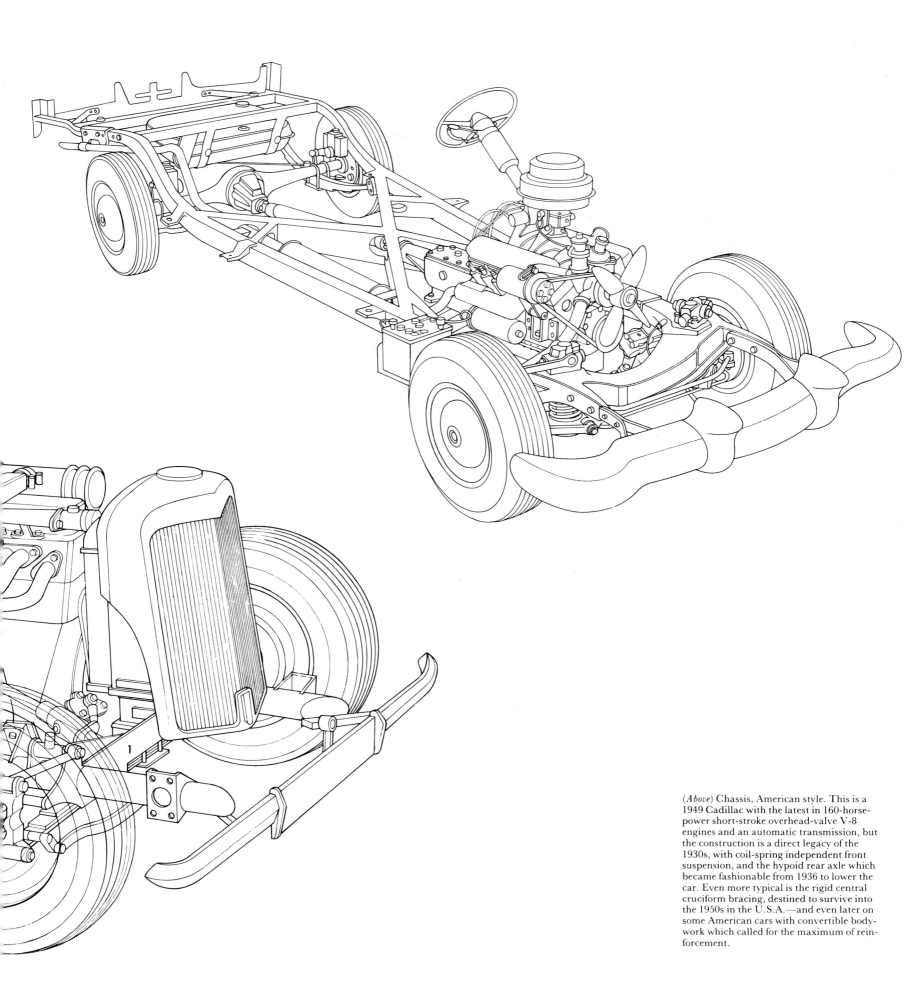

(*Above*) Chassis, American style. This is a 1949 Cadillac with the latest in 160-horsepower short-stroke overhead-valve V-8 engines and an automatic transmission, but the construction is a direct legacy of the 1930s, with coil-spring independent front suspension, and the hypoid rear axle which became fashionable from 1936 to lower the car. Even more typical is the rigid central cruciform bracing, destined to survive into the 1950s in the U.S.A.—and even later on some American cars with convertible bodywork which called for the maximum of reinforcement.

(*Top*) Some legacies of the 1940s—and of the 1930s as well, though in the case of the 1950 American Ford (*left*) only the side-valve V-8 engine, and its alternative in-line six, were common to the pre-war species. For 1949, Ford's chief engineer Harold Youngren had not only given the car a new skin: he had dispensed with the old beam axles and transverse leaf springs, in favour of independent coils at the front and longitudinal semi-elliptics at the back. The hypoid rear axle spelt an overdue farewell to that "high on its legs" look that had characterized all previous Fords, wherever made, and all seats were well within the wheelbase. The car looked very long, but it had only put on one inch (2.5 cm) over the superseded 1941–48 shape. It was also 240 lb (90 kg) lighter and had a lot more internal width for passengers.

The 1954 R-type Bentley Standard Steel sedan (*right*), by contrast, looked a true late-thirties motorcar, but was also largely post-war beneath the skin, though its independent front suspension had first been applied to a Rolls-Royce product in 1935, and the factory-built body (itself a post-war idea) followed closely upon the shape created by Park Ward for the stillborn Mk.V of 1940–41. The six-cylinder engine's combination of over-head inlet and side exhaust valves was common to all Rolls-Royce units in the 1946–59 period, and brakes were of the traditional Hispano-Suiza servo type as used since 1924, although now with hydromechanical actuation. By 1954, too, a Hydramatic gearbox designed by General Motors had replaced the well-loved synchromesh transmission with right-hand floor shift. The German Veritas Scorpion cabriolet of 1950 (*opposite, left*) had started life in the dark years of 1946–47 as a competition "special" using pre-war Type 328 BMW mechanics, including the twin-tube chassis. Since most of the bits were secondhand, even the Occupation

authorities could not really object to such a "factory", but by the beginning of our period the Veritas had acquired a five-speed gear-box and a new, seven-bearing overhead-cam-shaft engine by former aircraft manufacturer Ernst Heinkel. Specifications varied from car to car, but as much as 140 horsepower was available—and even with the "standard" 100-horsepower tune, top speed was around 105 mph (165–170 km/h). Reputedly Veritas lost about £1,000 ($2,800) per car, and the rapid renaissance of West German industry had put the little firm out of business by 1952. As for the Tatraplan from Czechoslovakia (*opposite, right*), with its *avant-garde* looks and a 2-litre rear engine, it was wholly pre-war in concept. The whale-like silhouette with central backbone frame, all-independent suspension, and air-cooled power unit (quick-detachable for servicing) had taken its bow at the 1934 Berlin Show, and this latest, more economical flat-four version had

been visible by 1938. Post-war cars had more power (52 against 40 hp), torsion-bar rear suspension (which helped the handling), and an unpleasing steering-column gearshift. The car would be the last Tatra sold abroad in any numbers. There was a lapse in private-car production between 1952 and 1955: when manufacture resumed, Tatra were back with rear-engined V-8s, badges of rank in their own country, not mass-produced. A development of this theme, the T613, was still being made in small numbers in 1983.

(*Opposite, bottom*) Yes, this car was actually made in 1954 and five years later you could have bought its twin from your friendly British Ford dealer for the £444 it was probably still worth as a curiosity in 1982. The recipe is simple: the 1932 Model-Y chassis updated in 1938, the body of its 1940 replacement (the Anglia), and the bigger 1,172-cc side-valve four-cylinder engine first seen in the Anglo-German Model-C Ten in 1935. Synchromesh, true, but not hydraulic brakes, while the transverse leaf springs at either end are the same medium which supported Model-T way back in 1908. Creature comforts were minimal, but anything is better than a bubble-car . . .

(*Above*) On the market in October, 1948, and still with us in 1970, to the tune of over 1,600,000 units—Alec Issigonis' Morris Minor. The Traveller Estate introduced in 1953 accounted for 204,000 cars. By 1966 it was beginning to look old-fashioned and cramped: it had had only one major restyle, in 1956, when it got a new grille and a single-panel curved windscreen. It had, however, gone through four engines, from a 27-horse-power 918-cc side-valve to the present 1,098-cc pushrod unit giving 48 horsepower, and top speed was up from 62 mph (100 km/h) to nearly 80 mph (128 km/h). The wood on these cars was both authentic and structural, a hazard to restorers of a model that would become highly collectable in the 1980s.

21

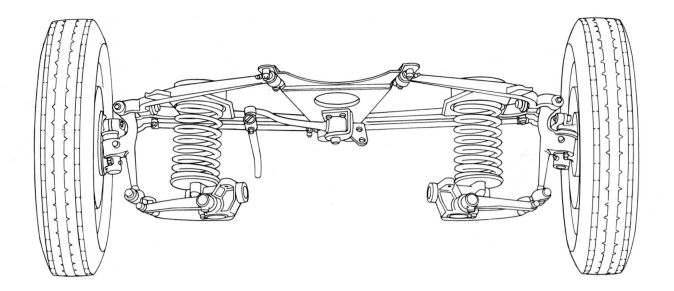

Independent front suspensions of the 1940s. General Motors' combination of vertical coils and short and long arms (*left*) was a classic, seen here in its application to the 1934 Oldsmobile, and still with many years of life in front of it in 1949. By contrast, 1949 Jaguars (*opposite, top*) featured longitudinal torsion bars of 1.32 m (52 in) length to reduce stress (*1*). A lower arm (*2*) projecting at a right angle from under the frame carries the stub axle (*3*), located by a forged wishbone (*4*). The lower arm is triangulated by a strut (*5*) running forward to below the chassis. This system was used on all of Jaguar's production cars—the compact sedans apart—until 1960.

eliminate varieties of style. Whereas 1934 had seen five body styles for the Austin Ten, and four for Morris, their 1950 counterparts—the A40 and the Oxford—allowed far less choice. Morris made only a unitary sedan, and Austin's catalogue included just a van-type station wagon although, for 1951, the separate chassis enabled them to add a sports four-seater cabriolet built for them by Jensen.

A strong legacy of the 1940s was the station wagon. Such a body had first been catalogued by Ford of America as long ago as 1929, and examples were offered by nine more U.S. makers by 1940, when Ford delivered 13,000 new wagons, and Chevrolet 2,904. These vehicles were, of course, the traditional "woodies", which shared nothing with other standard body styles and had to be built up like vans from chassis/cowl units. As yet, only Ford were prepared to work in wood—General Motors drew on three independent coachbuilders. In Europe, among those who listed wagons were Peugeot, Hillman, and Austin. Having been a specialist low-volume style before the war, it was no longer despised as a dual-purpose vehicle for tradesmen or, as in Britain, an estate hack for transporting guns to the butts, guests to the station, and servants to the village "hop". What really put the wagon into favour was the gradual elimination of timber, first for structural members and then for the whole vehicle. The pioneer all-metal estate car was the 1949 Plymouth, and henceforward timber became purely decorative, so that wagons could be processed through the factory's main body shops. We were still a long way from estate cars sharing most of their panels with sedans, let alone such dual-purpose sedans as the Renault 16 of 1965 and the Austin Maxi of 1969. But the trend had been set in motion.

Another novelty, the hardtop coupé, was barely visible at the end of the 1940s. Chrysler claim to have invented it on the strength of a few prototypes made in 1946, while the same year's Armstrong Siddeley Typhoon is a valid claimant, but what is generally accepted as the first hardtop—the Riviera—came from Buick in 1949. The recipe was quite simple: take a two-door convertible body shell and fit it with a permanent steel top. Thus, several birds are killed with one stone, providing a convertible's sporty lines without the endemic draughts, the short-lived canvas top, the relays needed for power operation, and a space-wasting well (often as much as 30 cm wide) which the top occupies in the down position. Hardtops also lent themselves admirably to two-tone colour schemes that broke up the large slab-sided masses favoured by contem-

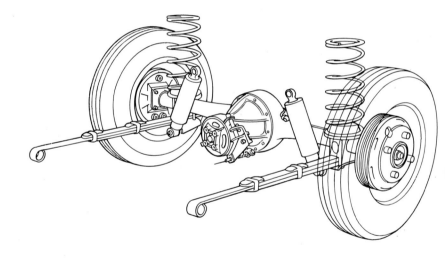

(*Above, centre*) Emergency brake, old style—albeit favoured by two big manufacturers, Fiat and Chrysler, throughout the 1950s. This rear end of a 1950 Fiat 1400 shows the handbrake drum on the rear axle. The use of a live axle and vertical coils is also noteworthy. Transmission brakes were exceedingly efficient, but the resultant "sudden death" stop could do terrible things to the back axle, and normally one used the device strictly for parking.

(*Opposite, centre*) Already known in 1949 was the disc brake, here seen as applied to Chrysler's Crown Imperial. This exploded view shows the double discs inside their finned two-piece housing. Braking action was achieved by forcing the discs apart, and the system was said to give 35 % more friction

surface than a twelve-inch drum, the biggest size of conventional brake viable with the 15-in wheel which was then standard equipment in America. Full enclosure meant protection from road dirt, but this early type of disc was expensive to make—so it was confined to the top of the Chrysler range, produced at the rate of a few hundred per year. Contrast the simplicity of Dunlop's 1956 disc brake (*opposite, bottom*), showing two pistons moving in a caliper attached to the back plate, and exerting pressure on circular pads in contact with the disc. The friction pads respond to hydraulic pressure, and high working temperatures require that the hydraulic fluid should be thermally insulated from the pads. Deep pads were said to ensure a working life of 50,000 km (30,000 miles), though about two-thirds of this was as much as the average motorist expected.

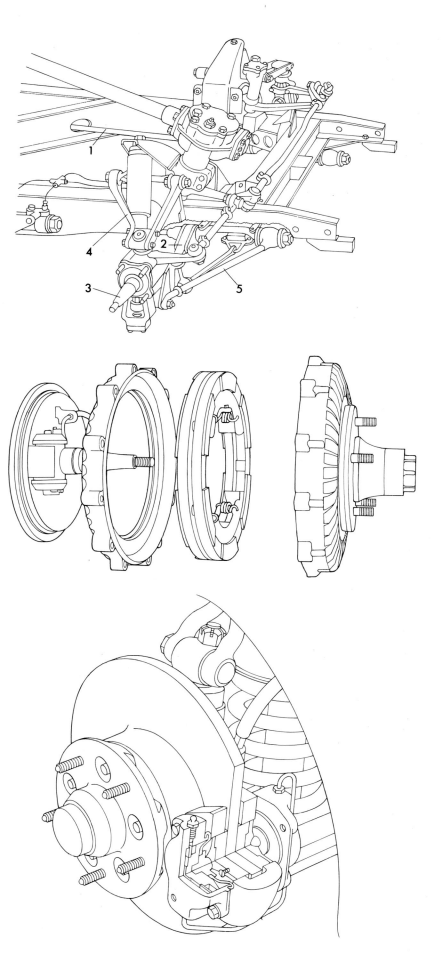

porary stylists. Better still, if the maker's range embraced a two-door unitary sedan, or even a four-door sedan, this could easily be transformed into a hardtop coupé with no loss of structural strength. Thus, by 1951, every U.S. firm offered such a style. It took longer to catch on in Europe, where convertibles were rarer as well, but outstanding early examples came from Hillman in Britain and Simca in France, although Fiat's Gran Luce 1900 was less felicitous.

Given all these advances, it may seem that by 1950 the only thing needed would be sufficient economic stability to keep the demand going. So what was required in order to bring the state of the automotive art up to the standard of the late 1960s, beyond breaking the stranglehold of the *système* Panhard? What did a car of 1950 signally lack from the viewpoint of a motorist nurtured on later machinery? Let us answer by looking at three typical models of that year—the Austin A40, the Peugeot 203, and the Chevrolet Styleline.

While all three seem hopelessly outmoded in appearance today, nothing archaic can be observed immediately under their bonnets, and one would notice their unsophisticated suspensions only after a drive. Synchromesh has not changed much, despite the difficulty of shifting with either the Austin's long and willowy floor-mounted lever or the Peugeot's column linkage. The Chevrolet is easier with "three on the tree", and its unsynchronized bottom gear would never normally be engaged. Brake fade, or trouble with the systems as such (hydromechanical on the Austin and hydraulic on the others), are unlikely. But the bother would begin with the handbrakes mounted under the dash, and the poor all-round vision due to thick screen pillars and small rear windows: wrap-rounds lie a year or so in the future. Only the Chevrolet offers a luggage boot of truly family proportions; accessory roofracks are desirable adjuncts on the other two models.

Once at the wheel, you would find it necessary to turn a key as well as pressing a starter button, since no key-starting exists outside America and even there it is not general practice. The European cars have electric wipers, but not of the modern two-speed type, and screenwashers do not always feature in the approved accessory list of this time. Radios and heaters are also extras (even if the latter are added for local sale in cold climates), looking and feeling like the bolt-on goodies that they amounted to—a fast downshift could land your foot in the heater fan, while the radio might bark the front passenger's knees. All automobile electrics were then based on the dynamo, and nobody had even thought about transistors in this context. Internal power assistance for seats or windows sounded as science-fictional as power steering: although this amenity in fact lay just round the corner, it was available only on American luxury cars. Automatic transmission was available for the Chevrolet, but disc brakes were virtually unknown. The Chevrolet is unlikely to have been riding on tubeless tyres, and these certainly would not be forthcoming for either of the European cars. Seat belts? One wore them in airliners when taking off and landing . . .

As for performance, the Chevrolet's 85 mph (138 km/h) from 3.8 litres may seem entirely adequate in our age of fuel conservation and overall speed limits. Even in 1967, a comparable cheap American six, the Plymouth Valiant, found 95 mph (152 km/h) hard work. But when accelerating, one notices the differences, as the Chevrolet takes 15 seconds to reach 50 mph (80 km/h) and the Plymouth only 9.2 seconds. With an average brake-pedal pressure, 86 ft (26 m) are needed in which to stop the Chevrolet from 30 mph (50 km/h), whereas the Plymouth managed it in just over 32 ft (10 m) even as a pre-disc model. The Austin and Peugeot have very similar general performance, albeit delivered in a quite different fashion, the Peugeot being taut to handle and the Austin wallowy. The latter's figures are, however, a true indication of the state of the art in those days. With a 1.2-litre engine giving 40

(*Opposite*) No, not a press shot from the 1939 Berlin Show: Adolf Hitler had been eight years dead when this first-series Mercedes-Benz 220 sedan was built. A new model for 1951, it was distinguishable from the last pre-war series only by its recessed headlamps and alligator hood. The all-independent suspension, hydraulic brakes, backbone frame, synchromesh gearbox, and 6-volt electrics were all legacies from 1939. But in place of the old, sedate side-valve six, there was a new four-bearing overhead-camshaft unit which offered 90 mph (145 km/h), easy cruising at 75 mph (120 km/h), and excellent flexibility. The column shift was, however, a particularly nasty one.

(*Top right*) The Daimler Conquest Century sedan of 1954–58 retained the classic fluted radiator and alligator hood dating back to 1904, and styling was authentic 1940s. Also present were a separate chassis and those good old British hydromechanical brakes, while until 1957 the preselective fluid fly-wheel transmission (regular equipment on Daimlers since 1931) was standardized, though supplanted on the last Centurys by an automatic gearbox. Handling was sure-footed, and the twin-carburettor Century was good for 90 mph (145 km/h). The basic Conquest was slower and cheaper. The name, incidentally, was an historical pun, dreamed up when the original price was costed out to exactly £1,066 (the year of the Norman Conquest of Britain).

(*Bottom right*) A familiar sight on British roads throughout our period was "Auntie Rover", alias the P4 sedan, over 135,000 being made between 1950 and 1964. Subtle and progressive stylistic changes passed almost without comment, although in detailed analysis this 1961 car of the 100 series looks very different from the original 75 with its central, Cyclops'-eye spotlamp. What started with four speeds, column shift, and a freewheel ended with four-on-the-floor plus overdrive, and engines fitted at various times ranged from a 2-litre four to the 2.6-litre overhead-inlet-valve six with outputs of up to 123 horsepower (in this car it gives only 104). Later examples, too, had front disc brakes and a servo, a far cry from the hydro-mechanical layout used on the original series.

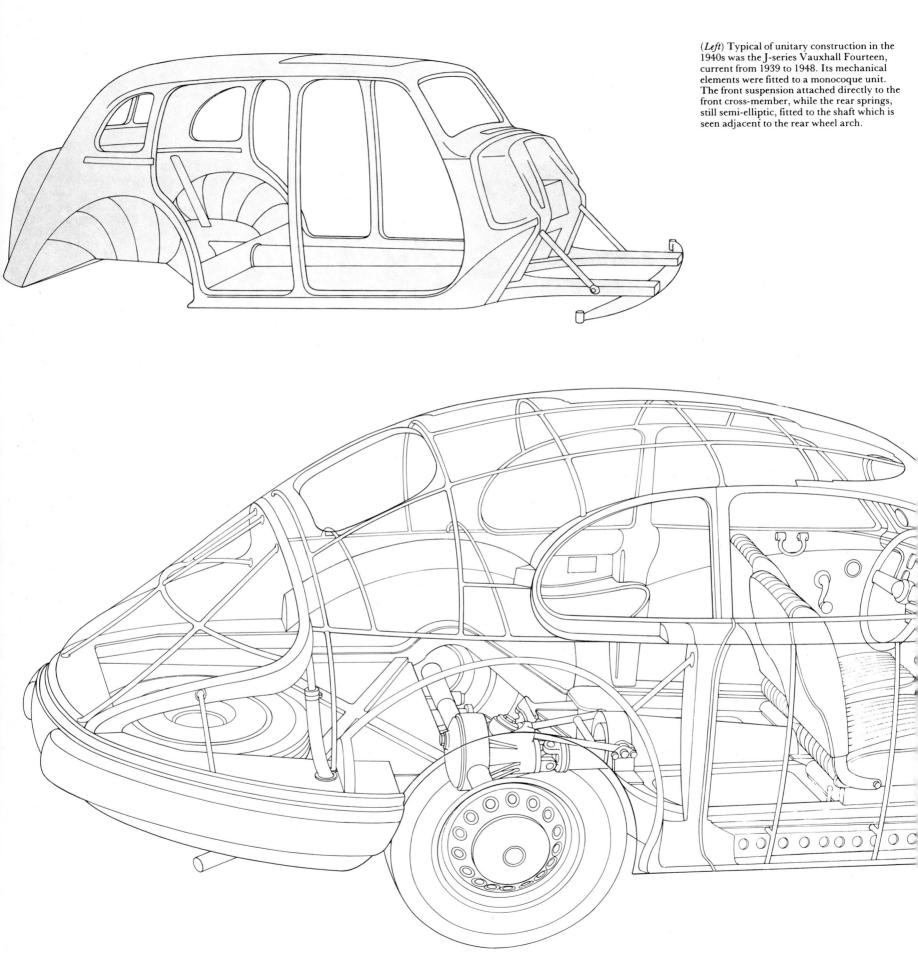

(*Left*) Typical of unitary construction in the 1940s was the J-series Vauxhall Fourteen, current from 1939 to 1948. Its mechanical elements were fitted to a monocoque unit. The front suspension attached directly to the front cross-member, while the rear springs, still semi-elliptic, fitted to the shaft which is seen adjacent to the rear wheel arch.

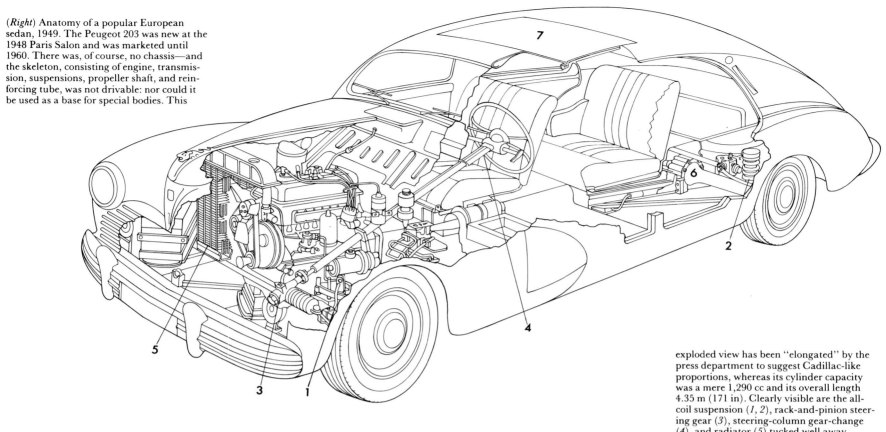

(*Right*) Anatomy of a popular European sedan, 1949. The Peugeot 203 was new at the 1948 Paris Salon and was marketed until 1960. There was, of course, no chassis—and the skeleton, consisting of engine, transmission, suspensions, propeller shaft, and reinforcing tube, was not drivable: nor could it be used as a base for special bodies. This exploded view has been "elongated" by the press department to suggest Cadillac-like proportions, whereas its cylinder capacity was a mere 1,290 cc and its overall length 4.35 m (171 in). Clearly visible are the all-coil suspension (*1, 2*), rack-and-pinion steering gear (*3*), steering-column gear-change (*4*), and radiator (*5*) tucked well away behind a heavy grille, although Peugeot had mercifully abandoned their pre-war practice of mounting the headlamps between grille and radiator. By this time, too, the worm-drive rear axle (*6*) was a rarity on private cars, Daimler being almost the only other user in 1949. Just visible (*7*) is an unusual refinement, the sliding roof, normally regarded as a British preserve, and one that was reluctantly sacrificed by Britons in the cause of dust-sealing for export sales. It would remain a Peugeot option throughout our period and beyond.

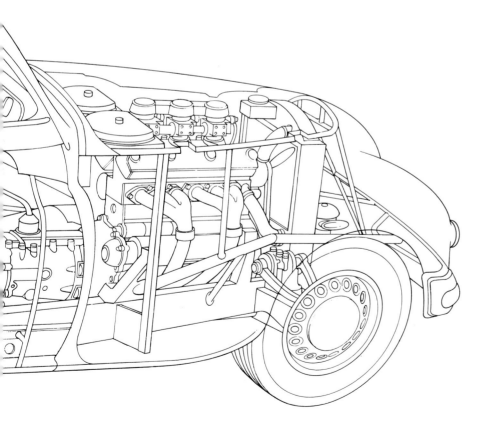

(*Bottom*) Advanced body construction. On the Bristol 401 (1949) the base design was the work of Touring of Milan (they had built very similar coachwork on pre-war Fiat and Alfa Romeo chassis), and featured aluminium panels laid over robust tubular-steel framework. Mechanically, this 1,971-cc overhead-valve sporting six-cylinder sedan was descended from the pre-war German Type 327 BMW, but aimed at a far wealthier market. In 1951 one paid £2,460 ($6,890), an interesting comparison with the £700 ($1,960) asked for a mass-produced British 2-litre like the Standard Vanguard.

horsepower at 4,300 rpm, it is flat out at 68 mph (110 km/h), attains 46 mph (74 km/h) in third gear, and takes 12.3 seconds to reach 40 mph (64 km/h), 20.5 seconds to 50 mph (80 km/h), and a laboured 34.8 seconds to 60 mph (100 km/h). The fuel consumption is reasonable at 32 miles per gallon (9 litres per 100 kilometres), but a leaden foot quickly brings thirst up to a less acceptable 25 mpg (11.5 litres/100 km). The car is light enough at 2,240 pounds (1,015 kg) and fairly compact, measuring 153 in (3.9 m) from stem to stern.

Now let us contemplate a new design from 1969, the Fiat 128. For all its front-wheel drive and transverse engine, it is barely an inch longer than the Austin, and there is far less wasted space. At 70 mph (112 km/h), it is faster in third gear than the British car is in top, and under favourable conditions it can be pushed to nearly 90 mph (145 km/h). A comfortable cruising speed is 75 mph (120 km/h), and even 80 mph (129 km/h) can be held although with a bit too much noise. While overall consumption differs little, the Fiat's 38 mpg (7.4 litres/100 km) on a long run could not be matched by the Austin, if only because such averages—say 65 mph (104 km/h) with a good proportion of motorway travel—would be excessive for the older car's engine, not to mention its chassis engineering. In acceleration, with the two sedans starting level, the Fiat would be doing over 40 mph (65 km/h) by the time the Austin had attained 30 mph (50 km/h) and, with the British car levelled off at 50 mph (80 km/h), the modern Italian would be running at 65–70 mph (104–112 km/h). Both cars could stop from 30 mph (50 km/h) in 30 ft (9 m), but the pedal pressures are interesting, the Austin's at 140 pounds (64 kg) being almost twice the Fiat's. Inflation, alas, renders accurate price comparisons impossible: the Austin's original owner would have paid £442 sterling, or half of what a Fiat cost in 1970, but against this must be set British import duty on the Italian car, whose home-market figure would have been at least 20 per cent lower.

The foregoing are only individual cases, however typical. We were still a long way from "world cars" such as Ford's 1976 Fiesta and its sequels. Model T had died in 1927 with no real successor. The Standard Vanguard and its contemporaries, mere restatements of conventional American compacts like the Willys Whippet and the Model A Ford at their zenith in 1928–30, represented a type that continued to engage the attention of designers, but it was doomed: too much car. The Volkswagen, although very much with us in 1950, had barely penetrated outside Europe. If relatively few nations were as yet producing cars, this was simply because industry needed time to get into full post-war swing.

National cars were being planned. In Sweden, Volvo had not become an international firm, while not a single Australian Holden had reached a customer outside the Commonwealth. The Dutch DAF and Spain's Fiat-based SEAT lay in the future. The supra-national J-cars, T-cars, and Fiestas would not descend upon us until thinking had swung firmly in the other direction, toward production of an integrated design wherever it was convenient and viable. That new industries were backed by the existing giants—America's big three in Australia, the British Motor Corporation in India, Datsun in Taiwan, and Fiat almost everywhere—did not in any way preclude the creation of local derivatives bearing only incidental affinities with the mainstream product.

Nonetheless, the structure of manufacturing had changed. In the 1920s there had still been good prospects for the "assembled" car, built up from standardized proprietary components: engines from CIME (France), Meadows (England), or Continental in the U.S.A., with Moss and Warner gearboxes, and Salisbury back axles. Identical elements were often shared by a diversity of makes and models, only the

28

(*Top*) Made in 1953, but essentially a car of the 1940s, is this Chrysler Windsor convertible. Unlike its more exciting stablemates, it still uses the familiar 4.1-litre side-valve six found (in essence) under the bonnets of its pre-war forebears, while chassis, suspension, and brakes are likewise little changed. The styling is warmed-over 1949 (hardly a banner year for Chrysler in this department) with the now-mandatory one-piece curved windscreen. Power steering is already an option, but only those who ordered after June could have anything better than a semi-automatic trasmission.

(*Opposite*) A shape in search of an engine. The Kaiser empire's "Last Onslaught On Detroit" (to quote Richard M. Langworth) did not fail through lack of good ideas. This Kaiser Manhattan sedan was built in 1953, but it had first been seen in the spring of 1950 as a 1951 model, and it certainly could not be confused with anything from General Motors' studios. You had built-in safety and an infinite diversity of colour treatments, within and without. Hydramatic, and—by 1953—power steering were available to order, but there was no V-8 to go under a hood that could easily have housed it: only a 3.7-litre side-valve six developing 118 horsepower. Hence the model-year's deliveries were a mere 27,000 units.

(*Bottom*) Common-sense five-passenger sedan, or—in this case—taxicab. Checker of Kalamazoo, Michigan, built this basic design from 1959 to 1982, with a happy disregard for all Detroit's stylists. This one dates from the late 1970s, but the only outward and visible sign of recognition lies in the heavy energy-absorbing bumpers. The engine, of course, is an overhead-valve Chevrolet V-8 instead of the side-valve in-line Continental six of early days, while the front disc brakes (offered by not a single American maker in 1959) are now standard. So are power steering and automatic transmission, though one pays extra for air conditioning. Further, in nineteen years the basic price (around $2,500 in early days) has all but tripled.

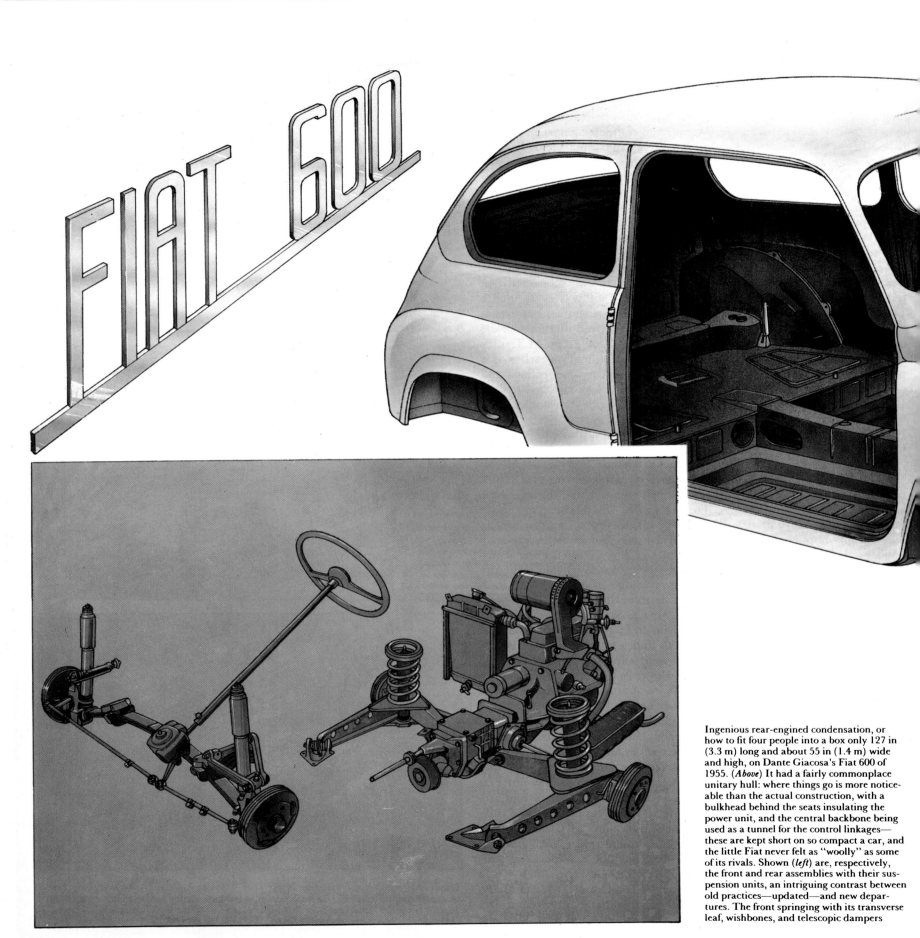

FIAT 600

Ingenious rear-engined condensation, or how to fit four people into a box only 127 in (3.3 m) long and about 55 in (1.4 m) wide and high, on Dante Giacosa's Fiat 600 of 1955. (*Above*) It had a fairly commonplace unitary hull: where things go is more noticeable than the actual construction, with a bulkhead behind the seats insulating the power unit, and the central backbone being used as a tunnel for the control linkages— these are kept short on so compact a car, and the little Fiat never felt as "woolly" as some of its rivals. Shown (*left*) are, respectively, the front and rear assemblies with their suspension units, an intriguing contrast between old practices—updated—and new departures. The front springing with its transverse leaf, wishbones, and telescopic dampers

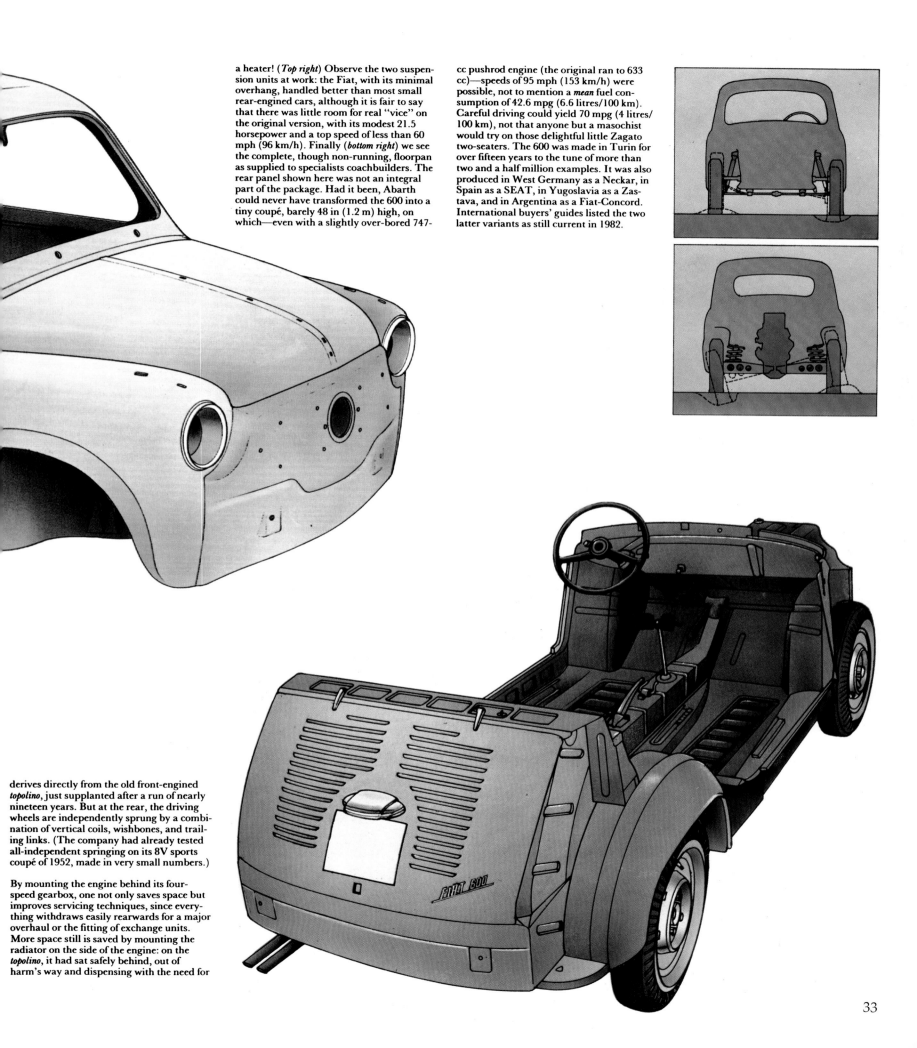

a heater! (*Top right*) Observe the two suspension units at work: the Fiat, with its minimal overhang, handled better than most small rear-engined cars, although it is fair to say that there was little room for real "vice" on the original version, with its modest 21.5 horsepower and a top speed of less than 60 mph (96 km/h). Finally (*bottom right*) we see the complete, though non-running, floorpan as supplied to specialists coachbuilders. The rear panel shown here was not an integral part of the package. Had it been, Abarth could never have transformed the 600 into a tiny coupé, barely 48 in (1.2 m) high, on which—even with a slightly over-bored 747-

cc pushrod engine (the original ran to 633 cc)—speeds of 95 mph (153 km/h) were possible, not to mention a *mean* fuel consumption of 42.6 mpg (6.6 litres/100 km). Careful driving could yield 70 mpg (4 litres/100 km), not that anyone but a masochist would try on those delightful little Zagato two-seaters. The 600 was made in Turin for over fifteen years to the tune of more than two and a half million examples. It was also produced in West Germany as a Neckar, in Spain as a SEAT, in Yugoslavia as a Zastava, and in Argentina as a Fiat-Concord. International buyers' guides listed the two latter variants as still current in 1982.

derives directly from the old front-engined *topolino*, just supplanted after a run of nearly nineteen years. But at the rear, the driving wheels are independently sprung by a combination of vertical coils, wishbones, and trailing links. (The company had already tested all-independent springing on its 8V sports coupé of 1952, made in very small numbers.)

By mounting the engine behind its four-speed gearbox, one not only saves space but improves servicing techniques, since everything withdraws easily rearwards for a major overhaul or the fitting of exchange units. More space still is saved by mounting the radiator on the side of the engine: on the *topolino*, it had sat safely behind, out of harm's way and dispensing with the need for

33

nightmarish. The minimum point for survival rose steadily from 5,000 cars in 1923, and 35,000 in 1939, to around 80,000 at the beginning of the fifties. Towards their end, a consistent failure to dispose of 250,000 cars per year was enough to render any of America's big three companies hesitant over that division's future. Hence the short, tragic run of Ford's Edsel (1958–59), and the demise of Chrysler's De Soto in 1960 after a patchy post-war record which exceeded 100,000 for the last time in 1957.

Independents, whether in the U.S.A. or elsewhere, had fewer dealers, fewer regional assembly plants in the large countries, and a higher unit advertising cost. Such firms in America needed to present a challenge in virtually every sector of the market in order to remain competitive. It proved too much for them to take on Buick, Mercury, and Chrysler as well as Chevrolet, Ford, and Plymouth. The Kaiser-Willys merger of 1954 possessed all the aura of a deathbed wedding. By 1966, the last remnants of Studebaker-Packard, another union from 1954, had gone to the grave after a short spell as a "foreign import" made in Canada. This, in effect, left only American Motors with the Nash and Hudson to rival the big three.

A similar picture is encountered elsewhere. Britain entered the period with her big six producers, backed by an equal number of "major-minors" (Armstrong Siddeley, Daimler, Jaguar, Jowett, Rover, Singer) outside the true specialist league (typified at different levels by Rolls-Royce, Lea-Francis, and HRG). By 1960, the Austin and Nuffield interests had merged, Rootes had absorbed Singer, Daimler had fallen to Jaguar, and Standard-Triumph had become part of the Leyland truck empire. Armstrong Siddeley were out of car-making, and Jowett out of business altogether except as a small concern supplying parts for extant vehicles. Nine years later, the huge Leyland conglomerate had gathered unto itself Austin/Morris, Jaguar/Daimler, and Rover—picking up Alvis with the latter, and terminating this firm's line of specialist cars after forty-seven distinguished years. Rootes were now just a cog in the American works of Chrysler. Further, subordinate makes of now merely sentimental interest (Riley, Singer) had been discontinued.

The trend was repeated in other countries. Fiat, at their zenith in 1969, controlled Autobianchi, Lancia, and Ferrari, while a tie-up with Citroën in France gave them a stake, although a short-lived one, in Maserati as well. In France, Chrysler owned Simca, and the hallowed name of Panhard—long a Citroën subsidiary—was reserved for specialist military vehicles since its cars and trucks had disappeared in 1967. In Germany, the struggles of the great independent, Carl Borgward, came to a bankrupt end in 1961. The closely linked Mercedes-Benz and VW empires now owned not only Auto Union (Audi) but NSU as well. Japanese mergers ran through the 1960s with the frantic aura of a speeded-up movie: thirteen separate firms were building cars in 1959, yet there were just eight in 1969 despite the successful intrusion of Soichiro Honda, a motorcycle magnate who achieved what the Kaiser millions had failed to do in America during our first decade.

Even where survival was permitted, the badge-engineer took his pound of flesh. This pernicious craft had its origins in a desire for greater coverage of dealers, as well as in cutting costs. Canadian Plymouths with Dodge or De Soto badges were a phenomenon from the 1930s, joined immediately after the war by Ford's Meteor (a Mercury for Ford dealers) and Monarch (a Ford for Lincoln-Mercury dealers). In New Zealand, Rootes invented the Humber Ten, a deluxe Hillman Minx, to gain a second import quota. At the level of sentiment, there were the incomprehensible permutations of Daimlers, Lanchesters, and BSAs in the middle thirties. Once again, a difference in name did not always mean a different product.

The disease was, perhaps, less prevalent at the beginning of our period. Engine and body rationalizations by General Motors and Chrysler in the U.S.A. were still aimed at preserving a fair degree of brand-identity, and GM's divisions still had their independent design offices even in 1969. Individual makes within the British Motor Corporation remained easily recognizable, although several of these shared the same engine by Austin, whose own interests were firmly in control of the old Nuffield Organisation by 1955. But the 1960s proved that uniformity had taken over. In England alone, Alec Issigonis' front-wheel-drive 1100 came with five different badges, the compact Jaguar sedan was also a Daimler, and the latest four-door sedan by Rootes—a lineal descendant of the Hillman Minx—could be bought as a Hillman, Humber, or Singer. To top it off, the little rear-engined Imp, while beneath the dignity of a Humber label, was considered sporting enough to be a Sunbeam on occasion.

2

POWER ASSISTANCE FOR EVERYTHING

The twenty years from 1951 to 1969 witnessed a vast explosion in the automobile business. World production rose from a mere 6,858,000 in 1951 to nearly thirteen million in 1960, and to a staggering 22,752,363 in 1969. Of these, over ninety per cent came from the factories of the top twenty companies, headed by General Motors and Ford in America, and by Volkswagen in Germany. Eleven manufacturers or groups reached the half-million mark, and another thirteen turned out at least 200,000 cars each. The simultaneous contraction in the number of makers and their offerings is almost as impressive. An absence of measurable falls in the U.S.A. and Britain is explained by the advent of the smaller specialists during the 1960s, which actually left Italy with thirteen firms rather than the nine she had in 1951. But in Germany and France, where the economic climate did not favour such operations, the field of producers shrank respectively from 17 to 7, and from 16 to 9.

Range structures also altered. With second-division competitors either falling out or being taken over, a major manufacturer had to widen the scope of his offerings. General Motors, leading America and the world throughout our period, listed seven makes and thirteen basic models in 1951, yet doubled the latter figure by 1960 and again by 1969. In 1951, there was one basic model of Chevrolet—and also of Vauxhall, though this came with an engine choice of four or six cylinders—whereas 1969 saw eight Chevrolets with nine alternative power units of four possible configurations: in-line four, in-line or flat six, and V-8. Capacities varied from 2.5 up to 7 litres.

To be sure, this trend was not consistent or universal. In Britain, the 1951 merger of Austin and Nuffield sparked off a great process of rationalization, a word in neither partner's vocabulary until then. At the time of fusion, their ranges ran to eighteen models, fourteen "chassis" including some unitary types, and fourteen engine variations, with badge-engineering confined to Morris and Wolseley sixes. Admittedly, there were three more models in 1960, but the new front-wheel-drive Mini had been badge-engineered into identical twins from Morris and Austin. The entire 1.5-litre sedan range had received similar, indeed more complex, treatment—further confused by the use of two separate chassis/body structures, one originating from Austin and the other from Nuffield. While engines differed in capacity, these consisted essentially of straightforward pushrod types, two with four cylinders and two with six. By the end of the 1960s, the process was brought to a successful conclusion. Its total of twenty-six models is less puzzling when we note that four were Minis, six belonged to the 1100/1300 family, three were

the bigger front-drive 1800s, and even the cheap Austin-Healey Sprite sports two-seater had an *alter ego* with the octagonal MG emblem.

Others were content to make what they could sell, forgetting the general-provider role. Renault of France, ranking sixth among the world's producers in 1966 and eighth in 1969, went through both our decades with just seven models, none of which ran for less than eight years, and all but two becoming million-sellers. Volkswagen built only air-cooled, rear-engine, flat-four cars from start to finish, although such a narrow policy was arguably hazardous: partly because the VW 1600, that "better Beetle" of 1961, did not represent the improvement it should have been, and partly because overall design concepts were already swinging away from rear engines. VW were also very late with the adoption of disc brakes—hence 1967 would see a 7.5% fall in their turnover, and a more alarming 16% drop in their export figures.

The VW situation highlights the grave dilemma confronting the car maker. Should he create a classic design and run it for twenty years for the sake of amortization, even at the risk of losing customers? Or should he swing into line with fashion, maybe too late, and then be stuck with the wrong design? Occasionally a latecomer succeeded: Chevrolet's Camaro pony-car arrived nearly three years after the Ford Mustang but soon caught up. By contrast, a promising contender from Rootes, the Hillman Imp, took an unconscionable time to develop, and was unveiled in 1963 only to find that BMC's Mini had cornered the market as well as setting the pattern for what would follow. That Minis outsold Imps by ten to one was not the real catastrophe, since Rootes lacked the production capacity of BMC even before the big Leyland merger. What did matter was that the whole Imp concept had become obsolescent by 1963, and totally obsolete by the time the countless teething troubles had been ironed out. Yet to have postponed the introduction still further in the cause of reliability would have guaranteed a failure. One cannot say categorically that the Imp killed Rootes, but it did drive them into the arms of the Chrysler Corporation, landing this empire with a headache instead of a healthy British outlet.

Here we also approach the vital technical issue of our second decade—where to put the works. This had never been a vexed question before World War II. Rear-engined cars were in the minority ever since the Panhard layout overwhelmed Karl Benz's philosophies back in 1899, while front-wheel drive had few adherents even in 1951. Of these, the British Bond was a cyclecar and not to be taken seriously, although the Citroën *traction* had found enough time since 1934 to eliminate bugs and train garage mechanics to cope with its idiosyncrasies. Panhard's

"We dig the Beetle", though in fact only 114,348 citizens worldwide did so in 1952, when this sedan (*left*) was made. Still, the next best-selling German car was Opel's Olympia, with less than 44,000 customers. Seen through modern eyes, the 1952 car appears austere and claustrophobic: on 1,131 cc and 25 horsepower, neither maximum nor cruising speeds were much in excess of 62 mph (100 km/h). Hydraulic brakes were listed on the "export" model from May, 1950, but this car won't have synchromesh unless it was made after September, 1952. By 1968, the 1600 TL (*top right*) retained the Beetle's basic and by now outmoded engineering, but capacity and output are up, respectively, to 1,584 cc and 54 horsepower, all four gears are synchronized, the front brakes are discs, and options include a three-speed semi-automatic transmission and fuel injection. This "better Beetle", stemming from 1961's model 1500, never really took the old car's place. Sales in 1968 were nearly 1,200,000 of the traditional series, but only 237, 617 of the 1500/1600 family.

(*Centre right*) The ageless shape—this Porsche dates from 1958, but it could easily be any year from the early fifties to 1965: the 356 series changed so little outwardly. Here was a car that took some learning, yet cornered 10 % faster than any of its rivals, could survive alarming accidents, and used less fuel than most of the opposition. Your 1958 car retained drum brakes, of course, but could be had with its VW-inspired 1.6-litre flat-four engine in two stages of tune: respective top speeds were 100 mph (160 km/h) and 109 mph (175 km/h). Nor were Porsches impossibly expensive—DM 12,700 in Germany, £1,996 in Britain, and 15,950 francs in Switzerland.

(*Bottom right*) By 1965, one would not think of launching an all-new 1,500-cc family car without front disc brakes, though one might offer a cut-price edition without them. Auto Union, however, fitted them to each and every Audi, all cars having pushrod four-cylinder engines driving the front wheels, and torsion-bar rear suspension. Maybe the choice of name was unfortunate (the original front-drive Audi Six of 1933–38 had been an expensive flop) but the new car caught on well, to the tune of 63,000 sales in its first full calendar year—and it was a timely replacement for the traditional two-stroke DKW, increasingly a victim of tougher exhaust emission standards. And if the first 1.5-litre Audis were a trifle lacking in power, this was rectified when the 1,696-cc version became available late in 1966. Note the *Vier Ringe* badge commemorating the four component companies of the original Auto Union combine—Audi, DKW, Horch, and Wanderer. Only the two former makes would survive World War II, though the Horch name was used briefly on cars (and trucks) in East Germany.

The original DKW-Front light car of 1931 had an east-west engine driving the front wheels, and so did its countless post-war descendants in several countries. Typical was the Bremen-built Lloyd minicar (*photo page 218*): seen here, in 400-cc form of 1953, is the power pack complete with transverse-leaf independent front suspension (*right*). With only two cylinders, of course, one could mount the transmission alongside the motor. Unfortunately, when makers of such cars (DKW in West Germany, IFA in East Germany, Saab in Sweden) wanted more power, they added an extra cylinder, and were forced to adopt a longitudinal mounting. The 1-litre engine from the 1966 East German Wartburg (*below*) was set well over the wheel centres with its four-speed gearbox behind (*see ill. page 141*).

(*Opposite*) Saving space with front-wheel drive. (**A**) The four-cylinder Volvo 122, a conventional rear-drive 1.8-litre family sedan of 1962, is 4.45 m (175 in) long, with plenty of legroom thanks to the hypoid rear axle,

but the propeller shaft still has to go under the passenger compartment. On the 1.9-litre 11CV Citroën *traction* in its 1934–52 form (**B**), the main advantages of front-wheel drive are a low centre of gravity and good handling. It is only fractionally shorter than the Volvo, is barely a five-seater, and has about half the Swedish car's luggage accommodation. The forward-mounted transmission is a splendid space-consumer. Renault's 16 of 1965 (**C**) still wears its gearbox in front of the 1.5-litre in-line engine, but the power pack is much further aft than on the Citroën, and the new hatchback body turns it into a useful load-carrier. A British contemporary of the Renault, the Triumph 1300 (**D**), is an altogether smaller four-seater with 1,296 cc, 3.95 m (156 in) long—but while a longitudinal engine is retained, the gearbox is mounted in the sump, Mini-fashion. Finally the classic BMC/Issigonis formula in 1962 guise as the Morris 1100 (**E**): east-west engine, gearbox in the sump, and the majority of its 3.68 m (145 in) length devoted to passengers and their baggage.

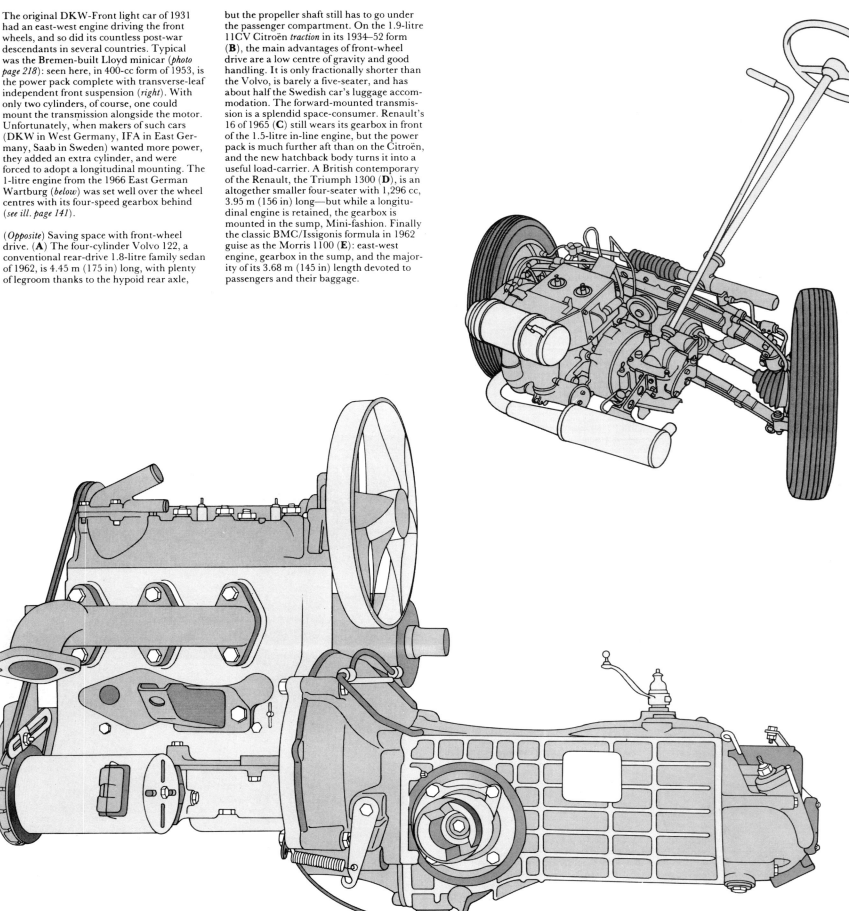

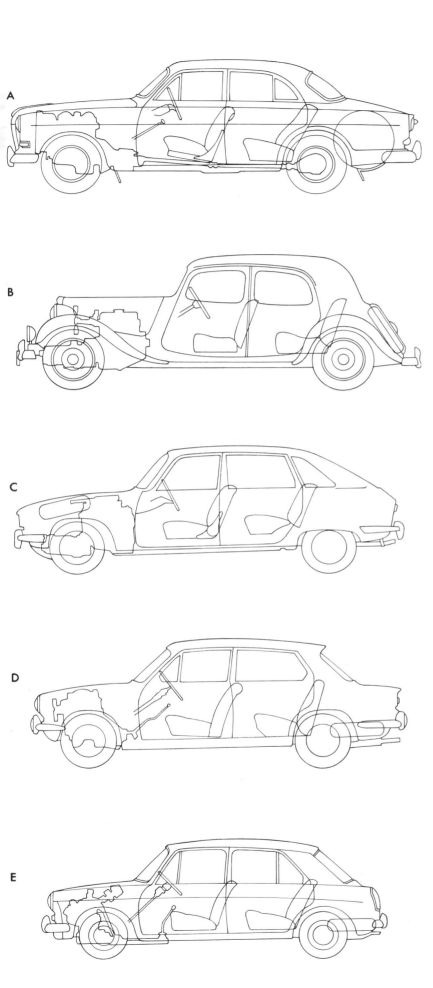

flat-twins, inspired by Grégoire, were newcomers and reached full production status during 1948. The Grégoire had already seen a somewhat chequered and obscure history as a proposed "people's car", with which other French, Belgian, British, and Australian sponsors had toyed.

As for the rest—the DKWs, Goliaths, and Lloyds of West Germany, the IFAs from the Democratic Republic, the Swedish Saab, the Aero Minor from Czechoslovakia, and the obsolescent Eucort from Spain— all were direct descendants of the transverse-engined DKW-Front theme first seen at the 1931 Berlin Show. Such advocates of front-wheel drive were old hands at the game, apart from Panhard whose model had a less than rapturous reception. Fast it certainly was, streets ahead in performance when compared to other miniatures. It handled well, and could win rallies: but it was rough, noisy, fragile, and cursed with a reputation for selecting two gears at once. To the end of its days, it would remain an enthusiast's car rather than a hack for the masses. Rear-engine supporters were even fewer, although two of their number, Renault's 4CV and the Volkswagen, were best-sellers. The only other serious contender, the Czechoslovak 2-litre flat-four Tatraplan, was produced chiefly for that country's Communist bureaucracy, some being sold in the West too.

The argument against the *système* Panhard, with its front-mounted engine driving the rear wheels, was that it wasted space. In addition to the assortment of mechanical elements at both ends, a propeller shaft ran down the centreline of the vehicle and intruded into the passenger compartment. Transaxles, on which the gearbox was combined with the differential, got rid of the gearbox hump but not the drive-shaft. The shaft might, of course, be made to earn its prominence by forming part of a backbone frame, as on some Mercedes-Benz and Lotus models. From the servicing standpoint, a complete overhaul meant a total stripdown, whereas with alternative arrangements the power unit could be removed and the remainder left undisturbed. Thus, by unbolting the front "horns" on a Citroën, the engine, transmission, and front end could be wheeled away. Yet this looked too simple in contemporary technical illustrations: the trouble was that, if you didn't want to take the whole lot off, the Citroën was not an easy car to work on. Nor, for that matter, was the rear-engined VW, with a flat-four engine set low and two sparking plugs awkward to reach.

Front-wheel drive as comprehended in the early 1950s did not economize particularly on space, either. The original DKW with transversely mounted engine was an exception, but more than two cylinders could not be set athwart the frame. When DKW and their disciples began the change to threes in 1950, a longitudinal arrangement had to be adopted, reviving the old problem. If you put the gearbox in front of the engine, it gives you plenty of legroom at the price of an extremely vulnerable power unit (a head-on collision means scrapping the car) and also of excessive length. The conventional 2-litre Standard Vanguard, a full six-seater, was 164 in (4.65 m) long, whereas Citroën's 11 Légère—admittedly a much older design—came out 9 in (23 cm) longer and sat five at a pinch, even if it looked every bit a car and its lower centre of gravity gave it the handling which the Vanguard signally lacked. The 2CV Citroën, with abbreviated flat-twin motor, measured 149 in (3.79 m) from stem to stern, taking up more parking space than did 800-cc conventionals like the Austin A30.

Equally endemic to such layouts were a wide turning radius and complex gear-shift linkages. The dashboard changes of both DKW and Citroën were confusing, although neither breed had as yet essayed a four-speed box. Memories of early front-wheel drives, such as the 1929 Cord, reappeared with headaches of weight transference and the big car's reluctance to re-start on hills. Further, outside Germany and

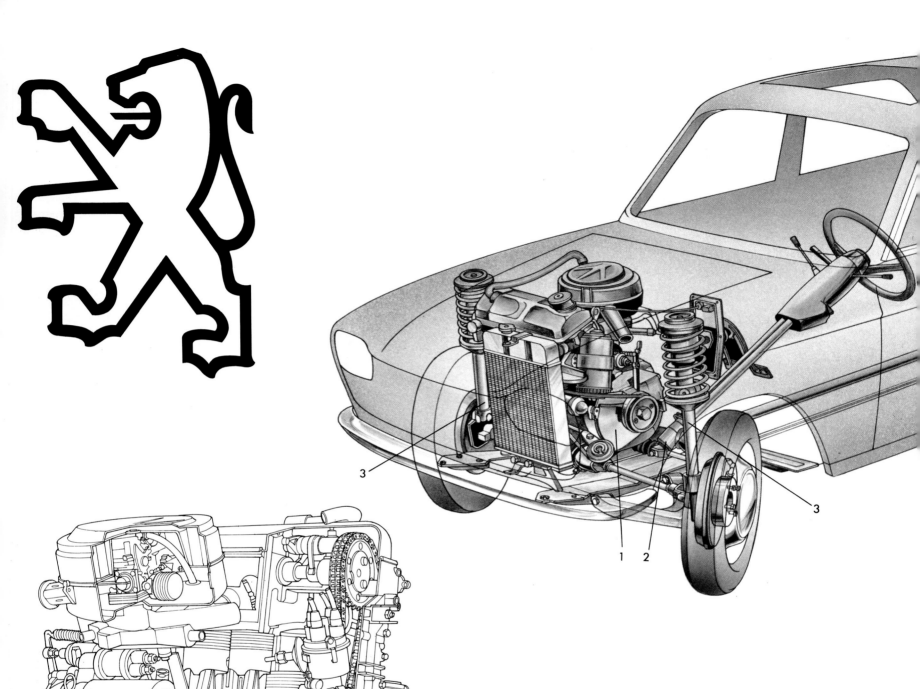

The Mini theme enlarged and developed on the French Peugeot 204, introduced in the summer of 1965 and destined to sell over 1,600,000 units in petrol- (and subsequent diesel-) powered versions. There were a coupé, a convertible, a station wagon, and a panel van, as well as the sedan shown in cutaway form (*above*). It was a bigger car than either Mini or 1100, with a 102-in (2.6-m) wheelbase, a length of 157 in (4 m), and a dry weight of 1,775 lb (805 kg). Seen here are the east-west engine of die-cast aluminium (*1*), the rack-and-pinion steering gear (*2*), front suspension (*3*) by McPherson struts and coils, and rear suspension (*4*) by coils and trailing arms, the latter pivoting on a tubular cross member. (*Left*) The 1,130-cc

overhead-camshaft engine is mounted at a 20-degree slant. The carburettor (at top) is enclosed within its air-cleaner to keep hood height down (a problem when the transmission is mounted underneath), and the robust five-bearing camshaft typifies 1960s practice even if it is still chain-driven. (*Top right*) A simplified diagram of the drive line, very much in the Mini idiom, shows the clutch output shaft running coaxially with the crankshaft, and in direct mesh with the gears on the primary drive of the four-speed all-synchromesh transmission. In the final drive unit (*bottom right*), there are double joints (*1*) at the outer ends to give a good steering lock, and constant-velocity inner joints (*2*).

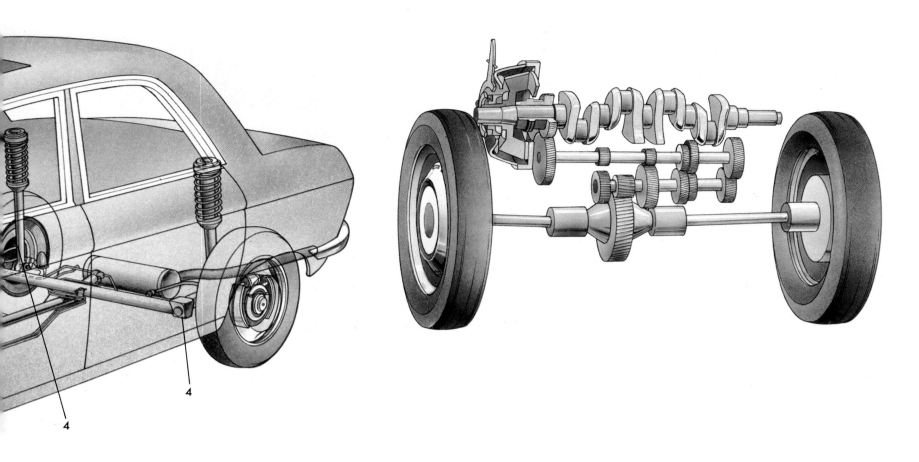

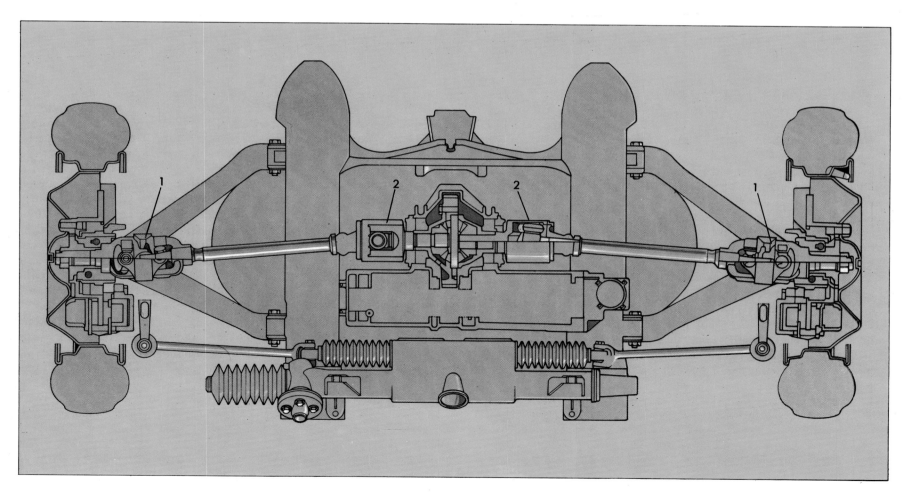

France, and their most consistent export markets, the public was not educated in techniques of driving with front-wheel drive. Another difficulty, associated specifically with the combination of two-stroke engines and driven front wheels, was that type of motor's tendency to "snatch": DKW and Saab incorporated free wheels into their transmissions as a palliative, which also gave the engine adequate lubrication on long downhill stretches. Understandably, then, front-wheel drive attracted few important recruits to its cause during most of the 1950s. No matter how revolutionary was Citroën's brilliant Déesse of 1955—it will crop up frequently in our story—it added nothing to this branch of the art, while Britain's Berkeley, a miniature sports car launched in 1956, was primarily an exercise in glass-fibre unitary construction.

The real breakthrough came in 1959 with Alec Issigonis' BMC Mini, which licked nearly all the bogeys of front-wheel drive at one fell swoop. It was more than just the original DKW theme brought up to date. By combining a transverse engine mounting with a gearbox built into the sump—and with a proper floor change as well—two extra cylinders could be added with no increase in length. The transmission was now farther away from the accident-prone front end than it had been on Citroëns, and the result was a full four-seater, 120 in (3.05 m) long, 55 in (1.40 m) wide, and 52 in (1.32 m) high. There was still room for some luggage, while such compact dimensions made the Mini ideal transportation in congested cities. A simple springing system with rubber in torsion as the medium gave a good ride, and the vexed question of steering lock was resolved by using wheels of a mere 10 in (25 cm) diameter. One certainly paid for this in terms of tyre scrub and heavier wear, but these factors were peculiar to tight-turning vehicles regardless of their drive arrangements: the conventionally-engineered Triumph Herald's famed "U-turn", appealing to housewives in virtually every English-speaking country, was no party-trick to be indulged by those who could not afford new tyres! Above all, the Mini was among the most forgiving cars to drive. One could even lift one's foot with impunity on the apex of a corner, something not recommended on any Saab or Citroën, and unwise even on the later 128 Fiat which incorporated many of the Mini's principles.

Others were quick to follow, notably Fiat with the Autobianchi Primula (1965) and Peugeot with the 204. Honda updated the old DKW transverse-twin theme in 1968, although using a four-stroke overhead-camshaft engine. Lancia's 1961 Flavia, a revival of the abortive 1948 Cemsa-Caproni, saved space with a conventionally located flat-four, while Ford of Germany produced a longitudinal V-4, this engine being adopted by Saab as well for 1967. BMC themselves progressively widened their range, continuing the Mini theme: the four-door 1100 came in 1962, and the roomy 1800 sedans in 1964. In 1969, their Australian branch managed to squeeze an in-line six across the front, although this did not reach Europe until 1972 and was never an unqualified success.

Longitudinal in-line engines still had some following, as being less complicated to service. The Renault 4, small and austere, appeared in 1961: like the later 16 (1965) and 12 (1969), it housed the gearbox ahead of the engine and managed to avoid extra length. But not until the end of our second decade did that firm combine front-wheel drive with a reasonably positive floor shift. Triumph on the 1300 (1965), and Saab on the 99 announced two years later, circumvented the gearbox problem by choosing a location below the clutch/flywheel assembly— the drive was taken forward beneath the block, with an integral output shaft in the final drive assembly. This cut down excessive length, but gave a more positive gear change than on other longitudinal layouts. On the 1.7-litre Audi (1965), Auto Union hung the engine well over the front axle centreline, with the gearbox behind.

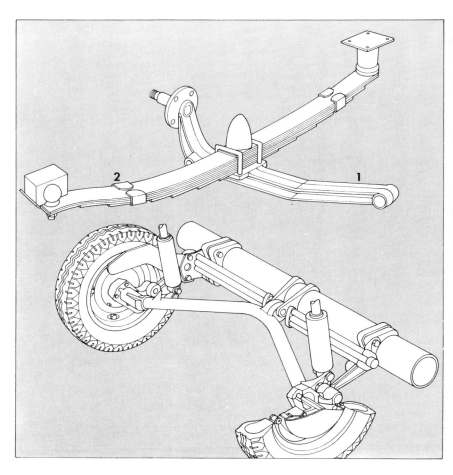

Really big cars with front-wheel drive had never quite succeeded. The 2-litre Citroën Déesse family as yet seemed to represent the limit of size. A predecessor, the 2.9-litre 15 with six cylinders (1939–55), had been too long in relation to its carrying capacity. It also suffered from punitively heavy steering at parking speeds, and a turning circle that would not have shamed a bus. Thus, in its later years, it tended to be the choice of vintage enthusiasts rather than family men. America, however, tackled front-wheel drive with a vengeance. Power steering and automatic transmissions were used to circumvent the problem of heavy controls. Further, there was a novel space-saving device on Oldsmobile's 1966 Toronado coupé, first of the new breed. A chain primary drive linked the V-8 engine with an automatic gearbox, mounted alongside the crankcase. The rest of the driveline was orthodox enough, but such a layout was viable only where overall dimensions were of secondary importance. In the Toronado's case, "short" was a relative term. Styling considerations alone dictated a formidable overhang at either end. Still, at a length of 211 in (5.36 m), it was 12 in (30 cm) shorter than a comparable rear-drive four-door sedan.

By 1969, designs with front-wheel drive had spread across the world. Major adherents included Audi, Ford, and NSU in Germany; Austin, Morris, and Triumph in Britain; Autobianchi, Fiat, Innocenti, and Lancia in Italy; Saab in Sweden; Peugeot, Renault, Simca in France; Cadillac and Oldsmobile in the U.S.A.; Honda and Subaru in Japan; and a few central European DKW-hangovers such as the Polish Syrena and the East German Wartburg and Trabant. NSU's marriage of the compact Wankel rotary-piston engine, front-wheel drive, and a semi-automatic transmission seemed to be an augury for the future. Two of these manufacturers, NSU and Renault, were recent converts from rear engines, while Fiat and Simca kept a foot in both camps. It was not lost

(*Opposite*) On front-wheel-drive cars, the rear end presents little problem, and some smaller and cheaper cars were simple in the extreme. Here are two from the late 1950s. On the German Lloyd Alexander (*top*), we see a combination of swinging half axles (*1*) and longitudinal semi-elliptic springs (*2*), the latter on rubber mounts. By contrast, the French Dyna-Panhard (*bottom*) prefers Citroën-type torsion bars as the springing medium, the wheels being supported on a curved dead axle. Both cars were powered by air-cooled twin-cylinder engines, the Panhard's—at 850 cc—being appreciably bigger than the Lloyd's 600-cc unit. The German designer, however, preferred a vertical layout with chain-driven overhead camshaft, whereas the Panhard's cylinders were horizontally opposed with pushrod-operated overhead valves.

The bones of America's first series-production front-wheel-drive design in thirty years, the 1966 Oldsmobile Toronado coupé. With a 7-litre, 385-horsepower V-8 engine, it was capable of nearly 215 km/h (134 mph). The engine is offset to the right in the frame to accommodate the automatic gearbox alongside. Also interesting is the perimeter chassis, which had ousted the traditional cruciform-braced type in America by the 1960s. From the forward end of the rear springs, the "frame" is technically part of the car's body structure. Power from the Toronado's engine passes through a torque converter and is then transmitted to the three-speed Hydramatic gearbox via a chain drive which is mounted on sprockets and damped by rubber.

(*Left*) Ideally a Mini should be photographed squeezing its way into a narrow slot between two Mercedes-Benz or Cadillacs. The grille pattern identifies this 1964 car as Morris rather than Austin, though this does not necessarily guarantee manufacture at the Oxford factory. The price paid for compact design was, of course, austere furnishings, sliding windows, door pulls resembling cheap clothes-line, and poor luggage accommodation, not to mention "dentist-drill" vibration when the engine was working hard in the indirect gears. But the result was safe, stable, and very forgiving.

(*Right*) There's no denying the compact functional appearance of the British Motor Corporation's ADO (for Austin Design Office) 16 theme, better known as the BMC 1100, with its interlinked Hydrolastic suspension and east-west engine driving the front wheels. Front disc brakes, too, were advanced on a small, cheap family sedan in 1962. In an eleven-year run, the firm sold a lot of cars, which included some 143,000 MGs that never knew Abingdon. MG customers got an extra carburettor (though not with the later 1300 engine), more speed, acceleration, and noise, a walnut facia, and usually (though not in this case) two-tone paintwork. Permutations were complex: on a left-hand-drive export 1100 (this one dates from 1966) you could have two doors or four, but Britons had to wait till 1967 and the bigger engine if they wanted the former layout!

Two cases of designs too late from Chrysler in Europe, though in fact the empire inherited ready-created designs from Rootes (*top*) and Simca (*bottom*). The Hillman Imp, here seen in 1965 form, was the cleverer of the two, with ingenious rear hatch and slanted 875-cc overhead-camshaft four-cylinder engine to Coventry-Climax design. But the original pneumatic throttle linkage gave much trouble, and a long teething period encouraged people to forget the better-than-usual handling and the superb, unbeatable synchromesh. Chrysler gave it up after thirteen years, during which sales failed to achieve the half-million level, even with the addition of badge-engineered Singer and Sunbeam variants. In France, however, they persevered with the Simca 1000 family (this is a 1970), unloading over one and a half million cars between 1962 and 1978. Like the Hillman, it had all-drum brakes in early days: unlike the Hillman, it had acquired front discs by the end of our period. Nobody liked its handling characteristics, but its fuel economy matched the Imp's, and the four doors helped sales along. Simca's technical links with Fiat are reflected in the fact that during the 1960s they tried the *système* Panhard, rear engines, and (from 1968) front-wheel drive as well.

Essentially a 1970s phenomenon was the mid-engine layout. This had become general practice on Formula I racing cars by 1961, and had been applied to a roadgoing sports car, the Italian ATS coupé, as early as 1962. By placing the engine well forward of the rear axle centreline, and inside the body, designers could not only reduce drag but also improve front/rear weight distribution. One may simply compare the 41/59 % of a 1960s Beetle with the more balanced 46/54 % of the 1967 Lotus Europa, among the few such cars to appear during our period. Others were the De Tomaso Mangusta, the Lamborghini Miura, Ferrari's first "small" car, the Dino (1968), and the French Matra M530 with V-4 Ford engine. For obvious reasons, mid-engine machinery was confined to sports models. There was room for at most two people, luggage space was limited and of awkward shape, and—with the engine just behind the cockpit—noise levels were likely to be high. This last factor was compounded by the final switch from open to closed sports-car bodywork, which coincided with the advent of the new configuration.

Nonetheless, the *système* Panhard was still firmly entrenched in 1969. Although General Motors continued to turn out their last Corvairs and offered a couple of "specialty cars" with front-wheel drive, they and the majority of their rivals were not yet ready for change. Nor, in principle, were the Japanese, the overseas branches of GM and Ford (the front-wheel-drive Taunus from Germany was on its way out), and such up-market makers as Alfa Romeo, Mercedes-Benz, Rover, and Volvo. If Renault were totally committed to "works" at one end or the other, Fiat demurred. So, for that matter, did Leyland in Britain, whose big 3-litre married the latest in sophisticated suspensions to conventional rear-wheel drive. Further, Leyland were about to make amends for their frenetic badge-engineering by separating their advanced designs with front-wheel drive (henceforth to be Austins) from a more orthodox generation of Morrises. They had little option: in England, the most consistent best-seller of recent years had been not the Mini or the 1100, but the straightforward Ford Cortina, without an original thought in its conception, yet reliable and cheap to service.

(*Opposite*) NSU's return to car manufacture in 1958 was based on a range of fast but somewhat noisy sedans with rear-mounted, overhead-camshaft, air-cooled engines. From 1964, the original twins were joined by a line of aluminium-alloy fours, all with synchromesh gearboxes incorporating an overdrive top. This is the standard 1200, with 1,177-cc 60-horsepower engine as current from 1968 to 1973. But as much as 70 horsepower were extracted from the smaller-capacity TTS series, capable of 100 mph (160 km/h). Nor was safety neglected. High-performance NSUs came with front disc brakes as standard, and all the fours sold in Britain with right-hand drive had these.

(*Above*) Mid-engined weakness revealed, on the Lotus Europa coupé introduced in 1966. The hatch on the rear deck, admittedly, lifts off, and routine items such as carburettors, battery, and oil filler are quite easy to reach. The original version with pushrod Renault 16 engine did 115 mph (184 km/h), and accelerated to 60 mph (100 km/h) in around 10.4 seconds. The cutaway upper body sides, spider-type wheels, and twin fuel fillers, however, identify this car as a later (1971) example with the 1,558-cc twin overhead-camshaft Lotus-Ford unit. 9,230 Europas of all types were built, the last of them in 1975.

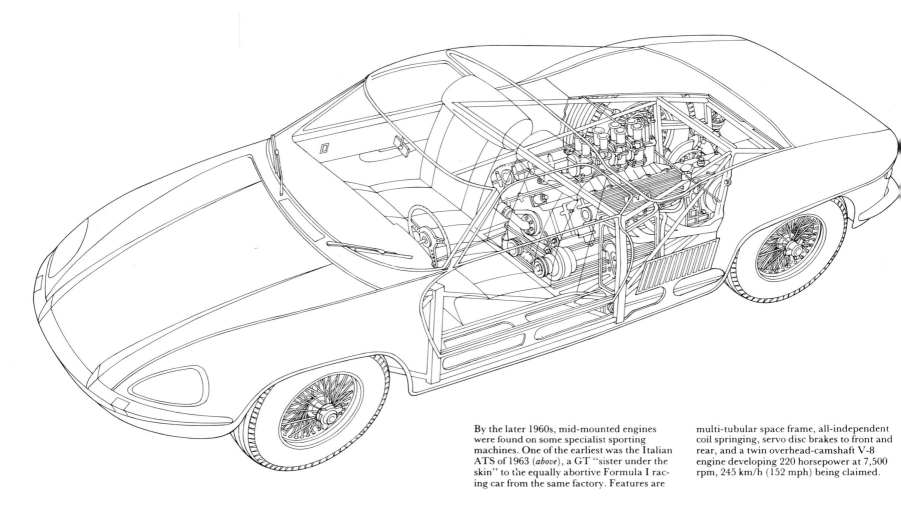

By the later 1960s, mid-mounted engines were found on some specialist sporting machines. One of the earliest was the Italian ATS of 1963 (*above*), a GT "sister under the skin" to the equally abortive Formula I racing car from the same factory. Features are multi-tubular space frame, all-independent coil springing, servo disc brakes to front and rear, and a twin overhead-camshaft V-8 engine developing 220 horsepower at 7,500 rpm, 245 km/h (152 mph) being claimed.

In 1951, to be sure, neither front-wheel drive nor rear engines represented mainstream thinking. We have already encountered specimens of that year's automobile: the stereotype remains to be examined. An average European model in the popular category of 1,100–1,600 cc would have a four-cylinder overhead-valve engine giving 40–48 horsepower at 4,000 rpm. It tended to have unitary construction, although some 25 % of the more important models retained a separate chassis— not so surprising when one reflects that less than half our sample was of truly post-war conception. Four forward speeds and column shift were in the majority, while a good 90 % featured synchromesh gearboxes even if none of them extended this refinement to bottom gear. Independent front suspension likewise commanded 90 % of the field (the Fords made up the balance), coils (59 %) taking precedence over torsion bars (23 %) and transverse-leaf arrangements (18 %). Beam rear axles were the rule, as were hydraulic brakes, the only exceptions being a few ancients with mechanical actuation and a couple of British models with the hydromechanical compromise, a dying legacy of the forties.

Few dramatic changes appear by 1960, but beam front axles have gone forever. The percentage of engines with oversquare dimensions has increased from 21 to 52, and their outputs are up, predictably, to a mean of 58 horsepower at 4,500 rpm. The in-line, pushrod engine predominates even in 1969, yet output rises again to an impressive 70 horsepower at 5,350 rpm. As for gearboxes, 65 % of the cars are back with floor change, 88 % have synchromesh on all four ratios, and no less than 47 % are available with automatic. Coil springing at the front is still a firm favourite (74 %) but the percentage of cars with independent rear suspension has grown in nine years from 12 to 41. Most important of all, 71 % feature disc brakes on the front wheels, and 15 % have discs all round.

The American car continued to pursue its own isolationist course. The form for 1950–51 was essentially that of 1939, except for automatic transmission and the opening bars of that V-8 orchestra which was to reach its crescendo with 400 or more units of horsepower advertised under the bonnets of 1968's muscle-cars. Where V-8s were not yet available, engines were in-line sixes and eights with side valves. However, Buick, Chevrolet, and Nash wore their valves upstairs—and all but the cheapest models of Ford had a flathead V-8, as did Lincoln and Mercury. Six-volt electrics, obsolescent elsewhere, were still customary, and would remain so for another three years, Cadillac and Oldsmobile leading the changeover in 1953. Americans, like Europeans in general, preferred the simple mechanical fuel pump to the electric type. Manual gearboxes, where offered, were invariably three-speeders, and the gearshift was on the steering column. Suspension arrangements were, almost without exception, a combination of independent coils at the front and semi-elliptics at the rear, although Buick and Oldsmobile headed the list of those favouring coils—if not independence—all round. Nearly everyone used a separate chassis, brakes were hydraulic, and steering was as yet unassisted, with a predilection for worm-and-roller or recirculating-ball systems. Cruciform braced frames, still widely employed, would soon give way to the simpler perimeter type, except on convertibles.

How many cylinders? Singles and twins were the preserve of the minicar, but Citroën and Panhard offered full four-door sedans with air-cooled flat-twin engines. In Europe, the four continued to stay

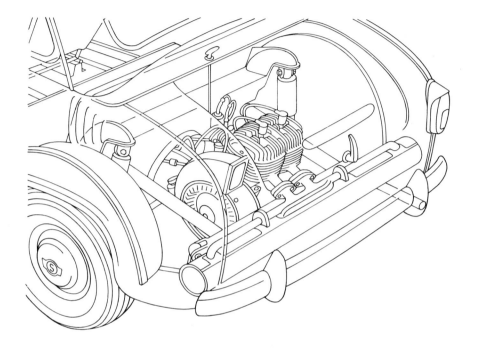

Horizontally opposed engines caused accessibility problems, especially with water-cooling, though on the Jowett Javelin of 1947–53 (*left*) the radiator was mounted behind. On this car, the side portions of the radiator grille were detachable, which helped. There was also a tendency for such engines to "drown" in freak weather conditions. Small transverse twins would fit just as well at the rear as they would at the front: the German Glas Goggomobil of 1955 (*below*) kept its engine in the "boot". Unusually for a two-stroke miniature, it offered full four-seater accommodation (*see photo page 215*), and in 400-cc form (250-cc and 300-cc versions were also listed) it attained 100 km/h (62 mph). Over 280,000 were sold, the last of them in 1969.

ahead of the six, powering some 42 % of the world's production types throughout the 1950s, with some small variations. By 1964, this share had gone up to 53 %, which remained about the norm for the rest of our period. By far the majority of these were water-cooled in-lines, exceptions being the air-cooled flat-fours of Volkswagen, Porsche, and their relatives, and water-cooled opposed types such as the Jowett (1947–54), Lancia (1961 onward), and Subaru (1968). The only new V-4s were the German and British Fords of the 1960s, although Lancia—who had pioneered this configuration in 1922—continued to build it right up to the end of their independent existence.

Poor accessibility was the Achilles' Heel of the flat-four. For the same reason, nearly all sixes were of in-line type. Porsche and Chevrolet, however, built opposed air-cooled types in the 1960s, while the V-6s of Lancia and of Ford in Europe were joined by General Motors, who began to take a fresh interest in compactness. Buick's first effort, also supported briefly by Oldsmobile, was launched in 1962. The day of the V-6 was to come. Sixes, however, came back slightly into vogue during our period, even though France, with her fiscal problems, offered no such engine after the demise of the 15CV Citroën in 1955. The watershed between fours and sixes was now just over two litres in capacity, with a tendency—especially in Britain and Germany—to use the extra pair of cylinders on prestige models. Classic examples were the 220s and 250s paralleling Mercedes-Benz' cheaper four-cylinder line, the 2.6-litre and 2.9-litre Austins with the C-type engine, the Kapitäns and Commodores of Opel, and the more expensive Borgwards. Apart from a short break in 1957–58, there was always a six-cylinder Super Snipe to complement the stolid Hawk in Humber's catalogue.

Sixes generally were moving up into the prestige bracket. Big fours were still viable in family sedans, but not in luxury models with a sporting flavour—as Armstrong Siddeley discovered to their cost in 1956, when they challenged the new compact Jaguar with their Sapphire 234. True, the Siddeley's styling was a catastrophe, but it handled better than the Jaguar and was nearly as fast. The lumpy feeling of that four-cylinder engine was the last straw. The pattern of four-versus-six, though, remained uneven. Rover, who concentrated most of their efforts on sixes, went back to an overhead-camshaft four in 1964 for their very successful 2-litre 2000, while Fiat tended to withdraw from the six-cylinder market in the later 1960s. The Humber Super Snipe ended a run of over a quarter century in 1967, while Alfa Romeo's 2600 and Lancia's Flaminia were neither of them impressive sellers. On the other hand, Triumph reintroduced a 2-litre six for 1964 and did very well with it, while BMW's overhead-camshaft family (1968) were to become one of the great commercial successes of the 1970s. A year later came a new 2.6-litre from Volvo. One that did not stage a comeback was the pint-sized six: the sole bid in this sector came from Triumph, who revived their 1931 formula of a small six-cylinder engine in a slightly lengthened four-cylinder chassis. The resultant 1.6-litre Vitesse (1962) was smooth and fast, but handled rather oddly. Nobody followed suit and the Vitesse soon acquired the 2000's 2-litre engine. The British fiscal system no longer called for such improvisations.

While the six moved up-market, the straight-eight quietly expired during the first four seasons of our period. Fashions in styling ceased to favour this impressively lengthy unit: the V-8 did the job better, thanks to superior sound insulation which eliminated its irritating "wuffle".

(*Opposite*) The European family sedan of the 1950s at its best—although both of these Borgward Isabellas, the sedan (*top*) and the station wagon (*bottom*), date from 1960. The overhead-valve engine and all-independent suspension were inherited from the car's 1934 ancestor, the Hansa 1100, but coils now replaced a transverse-leaf arrangement at the rear. The hydraulic brakes are to be expected, yet more sophisticated (even for 1954) are the hydraulically actuated clutch, the synchronized bottom gear, and the full-width styling. What, however, would have had four doors in other countries made do with two in Germany, which meant two doors on the station wagon as well. The steering-column change, unremarkable in the mid-fifties, was becoming a trifle old-hat by 1960, and the Borgward was a big car, 172 in (4.37 m) long and 66 in (1.7 m) wide. Isabella was also a bit heavy, at 2,253 lb (1,022 kg) dry, but in high-performance TS form she could cruise in the low 80-mph range (128–130 km/h). Still, for a small firm, full unitary construction was a risky venture and, though Borgward managed to dispose of over 200,000 assorted Isabellas in eight seasons, the money ran out for good in 1961.

(*Top right*) Lancia's Fulvia Berlina, made to the tune of over 190,000 units between 1963 and 1973. The firm had first adopted front-wheel drive in 1961 on the bigger Flavia, but this time they reverted to the traditional narrow-angle V-4 engine after the Flavia's Fessia-designed flat-four. The Fulvia's transverse-leaf front suspension, likewise, is a far cry from the famous "sliding pillars" first seen on the 1922 Lambda and retained well into the 1960s on older types. By this time, though, right-hand steering is reserved for British and Commonwealth markets. All-disc brakes are standard, and on this late (1971) example you will find a 1.3-litre 85-horsepower motor, five forward speeds, and quad headlamps.

(*Bottom right*) The V-8 remained the principal V-type of engine in use, though a successful V-4 was predictably the Lancia, still produced under independent management. This is the 1,091-cc power pack used to drive the front wheels of the Fulvia model introduced in 1963. It had twin overhead camshafts and was mounted in unit with a four-speed all-synchromesh gearbox.

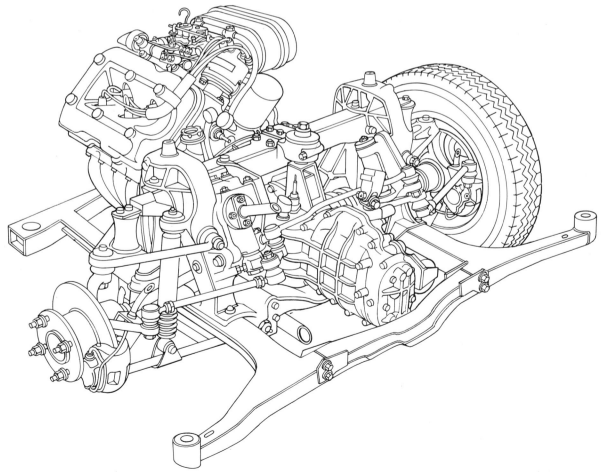

53

America's last two eights-in-line, Pontiac and Packard, were discontinued after 1954, leaving the Russian ZIS (a Packard derivative) to soldier on into 1958 before it, too, gave way to the ZIL with a V-8 unit. Our period also spans the golden years of the V-8 in America, during which the 90-degree short-stroke overhead-valve type swept the country. Cadillac and Oldsmobile were first in 1949, followed by Chrysler and Studebaker two years later. The other manufacturers had no option but to fall into line. Ford had an overhead-valve engine on sale by 1954, and 1955 saw V-8 Chevrolets and Plymouths.

The type possessed many advantages. Unit cost had been held to reasonable levels ever since Ford devised a means of monobloc casting, way back in 1932. The V-8 fitted conveniently into the space between two independently sprung front wheels, and width was not a factor which worried Americans. Better still, a short power unit meant that the same chassis and body could be applied to economical in-line sixes: in straight-eight days, one had to think in terms of two wheelbase lengths even if the two models shared a common range of bodies. As high-octane fuels came into use, the call was for rigid engines, and V-8s were rigid. Finally, four-throw crankshafts with five main bearings meant excellent balance. Early carburation problems were solved by using a single four-jet instrument instead of the twin-choke type with one half feeding an individual bank of cylinders. As for the V-8's thirst, this would be no hindrance until 1973's safety and emission drives.

The ensuing horsepower race merits a book in itself and, in any case, the remarkable outputs quoted were for engines running "bare" on a test bench, with no allowance made for power losses between flywheel and rear axle. But whether or not the figures were genuine, the progress was formidable. At the beginning of our period, 160 horsepower from 5.4 litres represented the norm. Then came Chrysler's "hemi" with 180 horsepower, and the race was on. By 1955, the hairiest Chrysler was good for 300 hp, and even the cheaper cars were available with "power packs" boosting output to around 200 hp as well as adding some 3 mph (5 km/h) to maximum speed, and lopping a vital 2 seconds off the 0–60 mph (0–100 km/h) acceleration time, the latter being very important in a country where overall speed limits were already in force. Chrysler were on top again in 1958 with 390 hp—one horsepower per cubic inch (16 cc)—and the ultimate was achieved in 1967 by Chevrolet, who were extracting 435 hp from their most powerful unit. Also offering over 400 hp were Ford, Plymouth, and Dodge. Even if these fantastic performances owed much to the advertising agencies, let us remember that the 1955 Chrysler 300 was a heavy car weighing 4,000 lb (1,800 kg), yet would top 135 mph (215 km/h).

There was little scope for V-8s in Europe, since the big-car market was modest and long runs were less than viable. Firms as well established as Rolls-Royce and Mercedes-Benz could afford them for prestige lines. But BMW's admirable 2.6-litre and 3.2-litre units were an unacceptable extravagance when related to sales of less than 15,000 units in a decade, and brought their sponsors to the verge of bankruptcy. The Turner-designed Daimler likewise had a ten-year run, but was dropped by a Leyland management already wedded to the Buick-based Rover and a design from Triumph which did not appear until 1970. One may dismiss the 2.3-litre Simca Vedette (1955–61) as a hangover from the past: it was merely an updated edition of the unloved "60" engine produced by Ford in 1936. Similarly, V-12s were reserved exclusively for Italian super-cars, their sole protagonists being Ferrari and Lamborghini. The Lincoln had disappeared in 1948, and the twin overhead-camshaft Jaguar would not reach the public until 1971. Whatever the motives behind the twelves of the 1930s, one may doubt whether Enzo Ferrari was in any way influenced by the ability of his early "street" engines to pull down to 7 mph (11 km/h) in top gear.

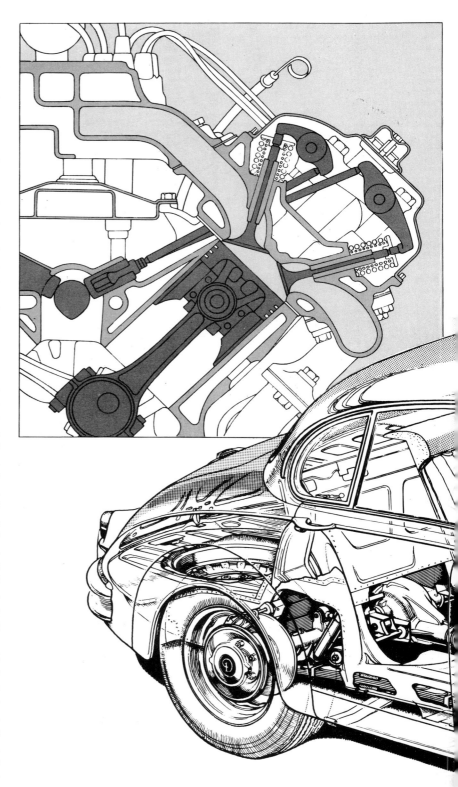

V-8s various. (*Top left*) The 1951 Chrysler Firepower unit (5.4 litres, 180 horsepower) was the one that sparked off the American performance race in the fifties, and was worked up to give double its advertised output, even if—as in the case of most U.S. motors—by no means all the advertised horses reached the back wheels. It had big inlet valves and excellent breathing, though the type was always expensive to make, and Chrysler Corporation's cheaper power units used a simpler top-end design. One of

Europe's few successful V-8s was the Edward Turner-designed Daimler, originally planned for the glass-fibre bodied SP250 sports car of 1959, but seen here (*centre*) in its most familiar application, beneath the bonnet of the 2.5-litre sedan (17,620 sold between 1962 and 1969). This was brought out after Jaguar had bought Daimler, hence everything save the engine was authentic Mk. II "compact" Jaguar. Initially, however, the Daimler version was offered only with automatic transmission. Far more complex was the 1951 Pegaso Z102 (*top right*), a 2.8-litre unit fitted to Spain's most exotic sports car, "a jewel for the rich" as its makers called it. Castings were of light alloy and there were twin overhead camshafts per block. In standard form it gave around 170 horsepower, although an alleged 285 were available with the aid of twin superchargers. The absence of a gearbox is easily explained: the Pegaso used a five-speed transaxle.

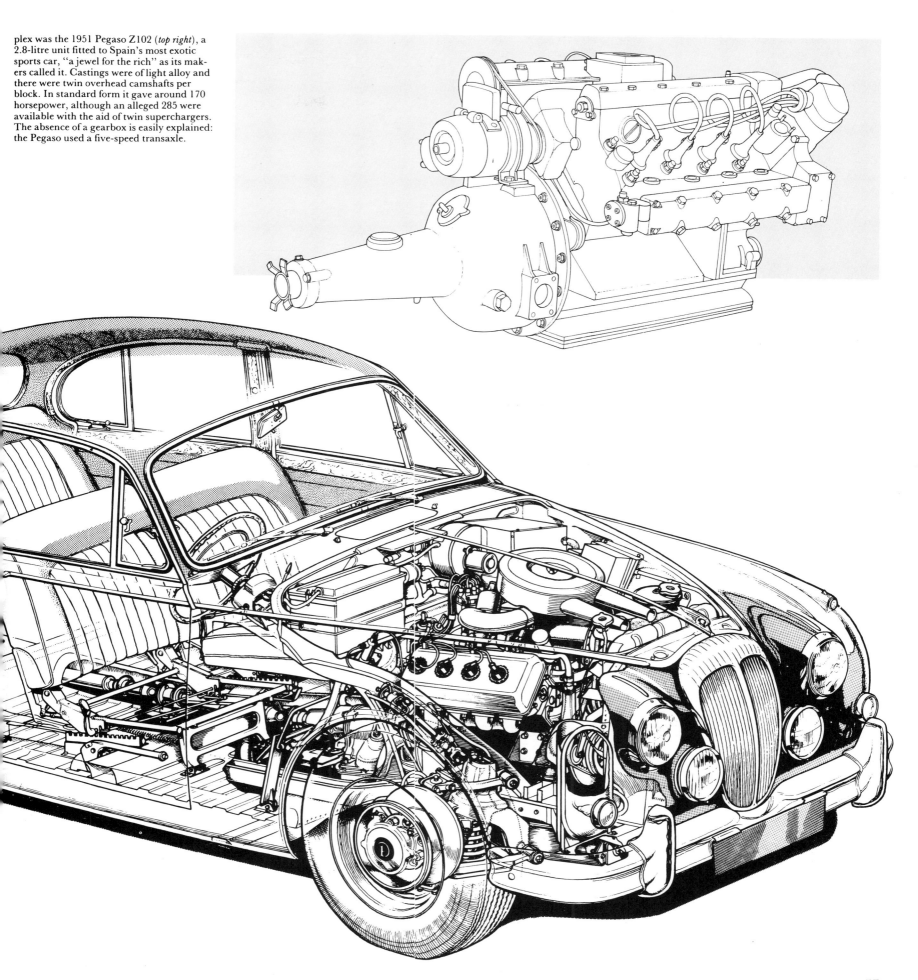

Alternative power remained only a talking point in both our decades. No attempt was made to commercialize an electric car. Diesels, however, had a modest appeal on various grounds. The fuel they used was untaxed in several countries, their fuel consumption was frugal in the extreme, and they would run immense distances between overhauls. Such virtues commended themselves to commercial travellers and cabbies. Less attractive was a high manufacturing cost, reflected in list prices, although by the early 1960s Mercedes-Benz had brought the differential down to a mere 7–8 %. Problems were the high-capacity batteries required to turn a high-compression engine over from cold, the unacceptable noise level, and the offensive exhaust fumes. The increased weight of a diesel could play havoc with handling if installed in a chassis designed for a petrol unit—the Fiat 1400D being a classic instance—while performance was lethargic. The limit for any diesel-powered sedan in 1969 was about 80 mph (130 km/h). Finally maintenance, when needed, was very expensive. Thus the market was limited, and the only major builder of such engines for private-car use was Mercedes-Benz, who had turned out over 600,000 diesel sedans by 1968. Others to try their hand in this field were BMC, Borgward, Fiat, Peugeot, and Standard, while diesel-powered 4×4 Landrovers were available from 1958 and, in certain Western countries, the Russian Volga and Moskvitch were marketed with conversions. Perkins, Rover, or Indénor engines were fitted in such cases.

An intriguing development of the late 1950s was Felix Wankel's rotary piston engine. It consisted of a triangular piston with rotational and orbital movements within a figure-eight casing, pursuing an epitrochoid path. The rotor or piston had three points of contact at the rotor top seals, which rubbed against the side of the casing. Thus, the spaces between the sides of the rotor increased and decreased in volume twice with every revolution. Such an engine, of course, dispenses with the crankshaft, connecting rods, and valves. It was also compact and

light: the original production-type NSU unit, regarded by German tax authorities as a 1.5-litre, weighed only 275 lb (125 kg) complete with all ancillaries. Except at low speeds, it was vibrationless, and one could run it up to an unrecommended 7,000 rpm without being aware of this. But alas, high machining standards rendered Wankels expensive to make, and their tolerance of low-octane fuels was not matched by other virtues. Fuel and oil consumption alike were high, and rotor seals were such a constant headache that, in later years, many Ro80 sedans from NSU were fitted with Ford engines. Only NSU and Mazda of Japan actually marketed the type, although Citroën, among others, indulged in long-term testing programmes before jettisoning the idea. By 1982, Mazda alone were still selling cars with rotary piston engines. The emission-conscious 1970s had taken their toll.

The gas turbine stalked through our decades as a chimera, never anything more. Tantalizingly simple, it had an air compressor, a combustion chamber to heat the air, and a vaned wheel in which high-velocity gases blasted continuously to produce the power output. Among its other attractions, an unfussy palate would burn such improbable fuels as tequila and peanut oil. It needed no warming-up period or regular oil changes, was lighter than an internal-combustion unit, and had 80 % fewer parts. Successful experiments were conducted in Britain by Rover from 1950 onward, as well as by Renault and Fiat. As early as 1956, Chrysler Corporation's experimental Plymouth turbocar was driven from New York to Los Angeles, the trip being repeated in 1962 on a later version. Chrysler went so far as to release 55 hardtop coupés in "turbine bronze" for assessment by selected private individuals under daily-use conditions. The idol, however, had feet of clay: building a gas turbine called for costly technology and metallurgy, while the best fuel consumption one could hope for was 13 mpg (21 lit/100 km). The irritating power lag of several seconds could be a problem, tailpipe temperatures were high enough to imperil curious pe-

(*Opposite*) Classically British, if with some post-war touches. The twin-camshaft high-pushrod four-cylinder engine of this 1953 2.5-litre RMF-series Riley sedan dated back to 1937, and its base design to 1926. Styling is essentially late-thirties, but there is independent torsion-bar suspension at the front, and later examples—from a run which ended in this particular year—had full hydraulic brakes (earlier cars had that great British compromise, hydromech) and hypoid rear axles. On 100 horsepower, 100 mph (160 km/h) were very nearly there, but the Riley suffered from the no-longer-acceptable beat of a big four-cylinder engine, and the steering was extremely heavy in town traffic. Sales of 8,960 units in eight seasons were nonetheless creditable.

(*Right*) Only those neatly slanted quad head-lights told the British motorist that the car on his tail was a Mk. I Triumph Vitesse (Sports Six to Americans) of 1962, capable of nearly 90 mph (145 km/h), and not the humble four-cylinder Herald. Planting a 1.6-litre six in the nose, allied to swing-axle rear suspension, resulted in handling problems, and there was as much (or as little) room as there was in the identically-bodied Herald. Unless the optional overdrive was specified, fuel consumption ran to a daunting 25 mpg (11 litres/100 km). In the early 1930s, Triumph's slogan had been "The Car That Is Different", and this was perhaps the kindest thing one could say of the original Vitesse, though of course front disc brakes were standard.

destrians, and the unit had a propensity for sucking in foreign bodies, with expensive consequences. In Britain, the development money ran out. In America, Chrysler's 1964 trials coincided almost with the first wave of Naderism, and the insurance companies panicked. Since 1973's energy crisis, nothing further has been heard of gas turbines for passenger-car use.

In conventional engines, pushrod-operated overhead valves were found on 65–70 % of all units throughout our period. The side-valve configuration, on its way out in 1946, was allowed to die with the old pre-war hangovers. Few new flatheads made their appearance, the most notable ones being the huge 5.1-litre six-cylinder Hudson Hornet (1951) and a redesigned version of the traditional 1,172-cc British Ford (1953), the latter lingering on into 1961. Other ancients destined to reach the end of the first decade were the Simca-Ford V-8 and the Austin-inspired Datsun, still around in 1959 as was the Austin 7, now made by Reliant of Tamworth for installation in three-wheelers. Chrysler Corporation of America were still making side-valve sixes in 1959, and continued these into the mid-1960s for light truck use, while the little 3-litre Studebaker Champion—a 1939 debutante—would not acquire upstairs valves until 1961.

Hemispherical combustion-chamber design improved the performance of overhead-valve engines. This was the secret of the famous 1951 Chrysler, and it also appeared on the successful 2.4-litre Riley of 1938–56, as well as on numerous overhead-camshaft models. Maintenance problems, plus the spectre of noise, discouraged the widespread use of the overhead camshaft itself on touring engines during the 1950s. Camshafts were still usually chain-driven and, in the early period, there were more defectors than new adherents to the overhead scheme. The 2.2-litre Morris/Wolseley family of sixes were never best-sellers and fell by the wayside after only 38,000 had been sold. Singer switched to Rootes pushrod designs in 1958 and Lancia, a long-standing user, also made the change to pushrods at the beginning of our story, in 1950. Probably the most persistent supporter was Mercedes-Benz, who brought out their successful 220 and 300 six-cylinder series in 1951, and spent the next few years phasing out the old side-valve hangovers from pre-war days. Coventry-Climax's small fours turned up in a number of specialist cars, notably Lotus and TVR, before being adapted to the Hillman Imp in 1963. Other notable users of the 1960s included Rover in Britain, BMW in Germany, and Willys and Pontiac in the U.S.A.

Curiously, the complicated twin overhead-camshaft engine had more initial impact. Salmson of France and Alfa Romeo of Italy had used nothing else since the 1930s, and kept this faith—the former until their demise in 1957, the latter right through to 1969 and beyond. Jaguar, whose 3.4-litre XK six with 160 horsepower had been among the sensations of the 1948 Shows, phased out the last of their pushrod designs in mid-1951 to concentrate on the newer type. Although their production figures (250,000 units by the end of 1966) could not match those of Alfa Romeo, the astonishing Jaguar soon proved its reliability with 250,000 miles (400,000 km) between major overhauls, besides its development potential of up to 265 horsepower on touring engines and more for racing, not to mention its versatility. Apart from Jaguar's own range, the big sixes went into Daimler limousines, racing cars and motorboats, armoured cars, and ambulances.

Twin overhead camshafts per block, on vee and horizontally opposed engines, were reserved for the super-sports cars, notably Porsche's Carrera series (1955 onward) and the fastest Ferraris of the later 1960s. Perhaps the most extreme case was the Spanish Pegaso of 1951, a V-8 with an incredibly noisy camshaft-drive by a train of gears, and with dry sump lubrication. With one of the very few supercharger installations catalogued in the 1950s, Pegaso claimed 225 hp at 6,800 rpm from

(*Opposite, top*) The four-stroke Wankel engine consists of an equilateral piston (*1*) mounted on a drive shaft (*2*), which it turns by rotating inside a casing with a cooling duct (*3*). The rotor points form gas-tight seals for three chambers (*4, 5, 6*). The working cycle begins (**A**) with a fuel-and-air mixture sucked through a duct (*7*) into chamber *4*, whose volume increases as the rotor turns. (**B**) The mixture in chamber *5* is being compressed at the same time, until ignited by a spark-plug (*8*). The combustion gases expand and force the rotor round. (**C**) The gases in chamber *6* have begun to leave through the uncovered exhaust duct (*9*) and are now almost gone. This chamber will soon move round to start the working cycle anew. (**D**) Two rotors are often used together for greater efficiency, mounted oppositely so that the engine will run smoothly. The combustion chambers (*10*) are partly sunk into the rotors.

(*Bottom*) In 1967, Mazda of Japan marketed their first Wankel-powered car, the Cosmo Sport coupé, using a twin-rotor engine of a nominal 1-litre capacity. Unlike the NSUs, it had a conventional layout, with a conventional synchromesh transmission in place of the NSU Ro80's semi-automatic. Front disc brakes were fitted, and a top speed of 185 km/h (115 mph) was quoted, but only about 1,200 were built.

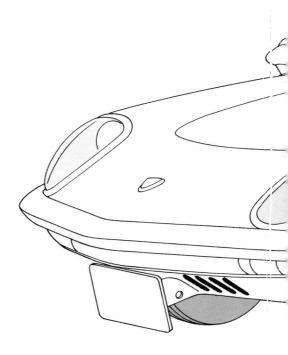

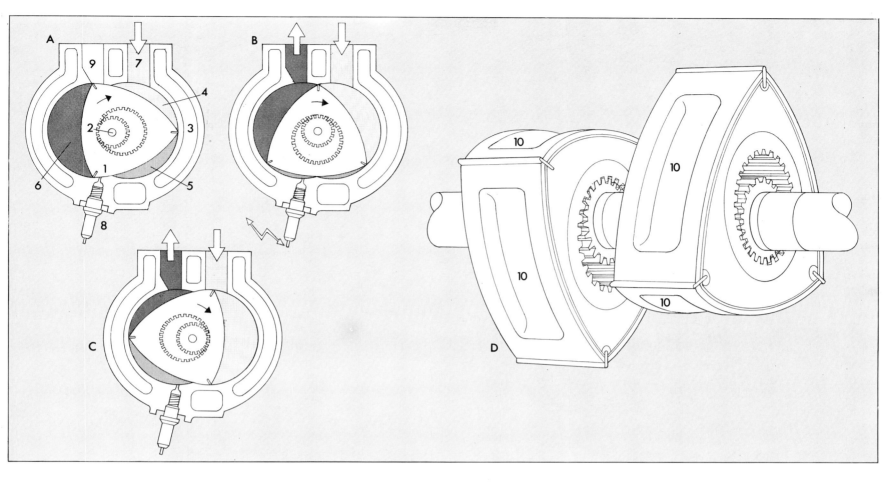

(*Opposite*) Solid Teutonic engineering: the 220S Mercedes-Benz sedan, 1957. This unitary version replaced the original separate-chassis type during 1954, and continued into 1959 without styling changes, though a lot of improvements crept in under the skin—servo brakes in 1955, an automatic-clutch option in 1957, and the SE series with fuel injection for 1958. The swing-axle rear suspension, as always, had its limitations, but output of the 2.2-litre four-bearing overhead-camshaft engine climbed steadily from 95 to 115 horsepower. For quiet cruising in the mid-80 mph range (130–135 km/h) the car had few rivals. Annual sales, likewise, were rising to around the 30,000 level by the late 1950s.

(*Below*) BMW "marked" Mercedes-Benz like an opposing footballer in the later 1950s, pitting a line of sophisticated V-8s against Untertürkheim's in-line overhead-camshaft sixes. Mercedes wouldn't essay a V-8 until 1963, by which time their rivals were struggling back from the verge of bankruptcy with smaller quality models. Their Goertz-styled 3.2-litre 507 (answer to the 300SL) was, however, a thing of beauty, and it could move to the tune of 137 mph (220 km/h) with the highest available axle ratio. The hydraulic brakes were servo-assisted but, although some surviving 507s have discs, these were never catalogued. Only 250 of these coupés were built and, after a skirmish with a Bertone-bodied fixed-head development, BMW finally jettisoned their eight-cylinder line in 1965.

64

(*Opposite, top*) The original owner of this 1957 Chevrolet Bel Air convertible probably paid around $3,000 (say £1,125) for it, allowing for freight and extras. Through European eyes, however, it looks an expensive car, all the more so for the elaborate grille, plated side sweep-spear, and fins which have yet to attain their ultimate in glory. With the top down, the aggressive effect of the dog's-leg windscreen is somewhat diminished, but the 14-inch wheels (new this year) hint at braking problems, especially with two-speed automatic transmissions and V-8 options giving 220 horsepower from 4.6 litres. As Chevrolet's only non-sporting ragtop in 1957, it drew over 47,000 buyers—more cars than Germany's Auto Union works sold during the whole season.

(*Top right*) From this angle, it's not apparent that the "works" of the 1964 Chevrolet Corvair Monza convertible live in the "trunk", or that the "hood" is reserved for baggage. Nor, as yet, had the crusading Mr. Nader vented his wrath upon this development of the Volkswagen theme with all-independent suspension and an air-cooled flat-six engine. It was, however, already clear that the car was more than a sub-utility compact sedan, and this year Chevrolet took a leap into the future by offering a turbocharger, using the waste gases of the exhaust to boost power. Until now, such installations were only seen elsewhere on heavy diesel trucks: their passenger-car applications would be a phenomenon of the early 1980s.

(*Opposite, bottom*) The 300 coupé of 1955 was surely the most exciting Chrysler in our period, though also one of the rarest—only 1,692 made. The recipe was simple: take Virgil Exner's long-overdue new shape in New Yorker hardtop form, lower it, give it the grille of the prestige Imperial line, and throw in a 300-horsepower V-8 with twin quadrajet carburettors, plus twin exhausts to make the right noises. Compulsory automatic and power steering might not add up to the European concept of a sports car, but then the so-called "muscle-cars" weren't competing against Ferrari and Jaguar. They would soon become a breed in their own right.

(*Bottom right*) Homologated stock-car racer, though it's still street-legal: the Dodge Daytona Charger 500 coupé, of which 505 were built in 1969. It is distinguishable from sedan offerings by the front spoiler, long nose with fully concealed headlamps, and a "tail unit" that would not shame a jet airliner. Power unit was the famed "426 Street Hemi", a descendant of Chrysler's original hemispherical-head V-8 of 1951. It gave 431 horsepower from 7 litres, and a four-speed manual transmission was regular equipment on this car.

from the category of 2–2.5 litres, to 1.5-litre sedans (Hillman, Ford) and even to the Mini by the end of our period. In 1969, indeed, among 132 major makers quoted in international buyers' guides, only 49 wanted no part of self-shifters. Notable holdouts were Alfa Romeo, Audi, Citroën, Lancia, Renault, Saab, and Skoda. All but the last-mentioned would soon give in to this ubiquitous pain-killer.

The main casualties of the automatic revolution were, of course, the semi-automatic systems. Chrysler's Fluidrive had given way to a proper automatic by 1954, while preselectors also became part of history. The electrically selected Cotal died because its principal French customers went out of business, and the same went for the Wilsons favoured by Talbot in France and Armstrong Siddeley in Britain. The latter firm, like Daimler, had in any case switched to proprietary automatics as being cheaper and less complicated. Armstrong Siddeley flirted briefly with electric selection of the gears in 1953–55, and another electric, the German Getrag used on the miniature Goggomobil in 1957, was an ingenious device actuated by a tiny lever. Sadly, this system did not work in bottom gear, and often expired altogether.

Automatic clutches flitted briefly across the scene in the later 1950s. Notable specimens were Renault's Ferlec, the German Saxomat offered on a diversity of makes, and the Lockheed Manumatic in Britain. On these, an electric switch, usually built into the gear-shift knob, disengaged the clutch when the lever was moved. Their balance could be upset by fast idling speeds with the engine running at low temperature. In fact, the auto-clutch was only a palliative to keep the manufacturers alive until small engines could be made powerful enough to absorb the inherent power losses of automatic transmission. Such arrangements were still around in the late sixties. On NSU's Ro80, driver-controlled manual selection was successfully combined with a torque converter, and Porsche used a rather similar device on their "Sporto-

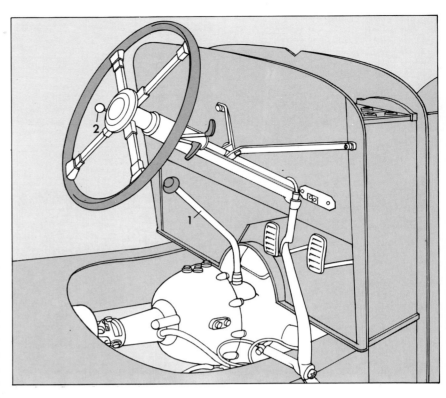

(*Top*) Complicated shifting. Still with us in the early fifties was the Cotal electromagnetic gear change, which used two levers: a floor-mounted forward/reverse selector (*1*), and a tiny finger-type gate (*2*) which selected the individual ratios electrically and, inci-

dentally, offered four speeds in the wrong direction to the foolhardy. This picture shows a Salmson of the 1940s, but the Cotal's most dedicated users—Delahaye and Delage—favoured a smaller and neater floor lever.

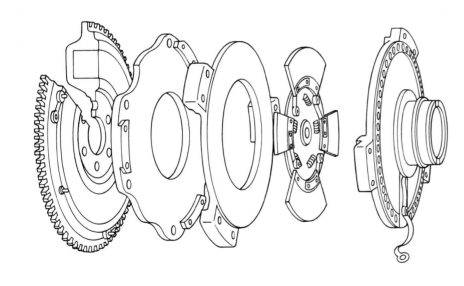

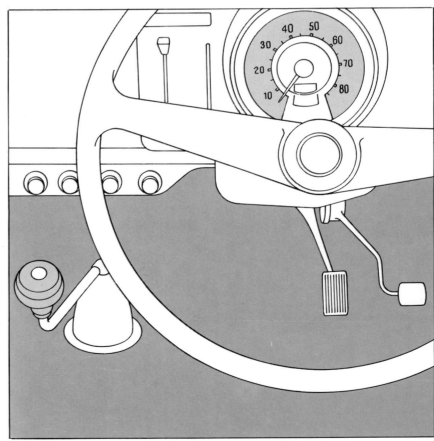

Painless, if not automatic, shifting—with full driver control. Two from the 1955–57 period were (*above*) the Ferlec electromagnetic clutch offered on Renault and some other French makes, and (*right*) Standard's Standrive as available on that company's small sedans. The French arrangement, seen here in exploded form, dispensed with a clutch pedal. Engagement was automatic, via cur-

rent from the dynamo as the engine was accelerated, and disengagement was equally automatic, being controlled by movement of the gear lever. On the small 4CV, it cost only about £30 ($85) extra. The dynamo also powered Standrive, although disengagement of the clutch was obtained by pressing the button on the gear-lever knob.

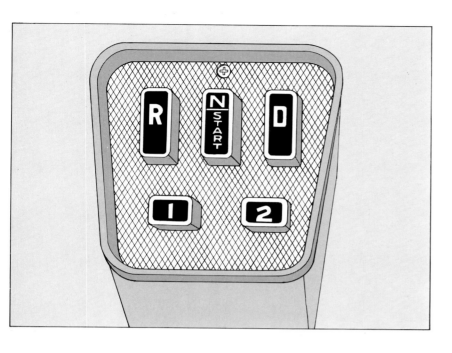

Automatic meant column-mounted selectors in the 1940s. Not so always in the fifties and sixties. The 1957 Dodge (*above*) and other contemporary Chrysler Corporation products used "pushbutton Torque-Flite", a self-explanatory device mounted to the driver's left on this left-hand-drive car. A year later, Ford's ill-fated Edsel featured what its makers called "Teletouch", with the buttons (*bottom left*) in the centre of the steering-wheel boss, a component which fortunately did not rotate with the wheel. By 1967 the trend was, however, towards a floor-mounted in-line quadrant (*bottom right*), here seen on Chevrolet's Corvette sports car. This had the advantage that the same centre console (and therefore the same sheet metal) could be used on cars fitted with "four on the floor" (four-speed manual).

matic" option. Fiat's Idroconvert was an old-fashioned automatic clutch, viable in Italy where people were wary of automatics.

Also a casualty was the three-speed manual box, a victim of the more sophisticated automatics. It survived on a modest scale in America, and on medium-sized American-type sedans (Austin, Datsun, Ford, Holden, Vauxhall) made elsewhere, usually in association with column-shift. This abomination reached its zenith in the first years of our period, when even sports cars (Jowett Jupiter, early DB2 Aston Martins) were thus afflicted. Its stronghold, apart from the U.S.A., was Germany. Yet it died, largely because of the virtual impossibility of arranging five gears (including reverse) in a vertical plane without the need for unnatural movements. Devious linkages encouraged wear in the selectors: hence the tiresome "two-finger exercises" familiar to all who have tried to hold an aged Hillman Minx in second gear. When the pony-car craze swept America in 1964, the public suddenly took an interest in manual boxes and, significantly, Detroit—back with four speeds for the first time in over thirty years—was careful to place the lever firmly on the floor and keep it there. On the other hand, the early five-speeders of Fiat and Alfa Romeo (1953–55) were column-selected, and one American critic summarized the 1900C Alfa as having "the most godawful shift ever made".

All-synchromesh boxes were, by contrast, a phenomenon of the sixties. True, by 1935 it was possible to buy an Adler, an Alvis, or even a Hillman Minx for £165, with such equipment. But high manufacturing costs, and—in the Hillman's case—a remarkable ability to "hang on" in top gear, defeated the object. After 1938, Hillman owners went back to double-declutching in and out of bottom gear, and they probably did not notice the difference. Be that as it may, the general rule in 1951 was to synchronize all forward gears save first. Main exceptions were the Standard Vanguard and the all-new six-cylinder Mercedes-Benz range.

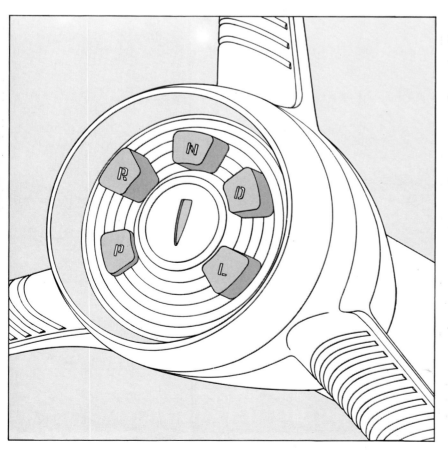

(*Opposite*) "We are a poor country," said Pegaso's chief engineer Wilfredo Ricart, "and therefore we must make jewels for the rich." This Z102B made in the old Hispano-Suiza factory at Barcelona in 1954 is certainly exotic: four-cam, 3.2-litre alloy V-8 engine, four carburettors, five-speed non-synchromesh transaxle of de Dion type, limited-slip differential, and inboard rear brakes. Saoutchik of Paris and Touring of Milan produced bodies to suit—this example is by the latter firm and could well have

inspired both the E-type Jaguar (1961) and the Z-series Datsun (1969). A $30,000 list price was mentioned in the U.S.A., which explains why only 125 Pegasos were made between 1951 and 1958.

(*Below*) Bubble-car heresy, or the one that preferred a four-stroke engine, in this case a 198-cc single. Heinkel, makers of this *Kabinenroller* (introduced in 1956) made such a unit and fitted it to their own cars. Here we see the British-built 1962 edition from

Trojan with its front door open to show the interior. Unlike BMW with the Isetta, Heinkel kept the steering separate from this door and saved themselves some complicated linkages. The first cars had two close-set rear wheels, but in Britain, where both sales and road tax concessions favoured the three-wheeler, this latter version was more popular. Even on the smallest cars, the Germans liked the cabrio-limousine style. Trojan accounted for over 10,000 of the 200s, more than were sold in Germany.

30 mph (50 km/h) and 2.8 seconds quicker to 60 mph (100 km/h), while fuel consumption increased significantly from 27.3 to 24.8 mpg (10.6 to 11.4 litres/100 km). On the Continent itself, small automatic-equipped cars took longer to arrive. Automatic Fords from Cologne were on sale by 1965. Opel, after an interval with automatic clutches, offered GM-built boxes on their six-cylinder cars in 1961, extending the option to their intermediate range in 1968. BMW adopted the ZF box in 1966, and Volkswagen had a rather inefficient three-speed "stick automatic" which sold well in America but was unpopular elsewhere.

A revolution in braking methods also characterized our twenty years. Statistical samples can be misleading, since they vary according to parameters: either the number of cars made, or the different types on the market. It would, therefore, be unfair to claim wholesale acceptance of hydraulic systems in 1938, when at least four of the world's biggest manufacturers—Austin, Ford, Peugeot, and Renault—were still firmly committed to rods or cables. But the latter arrangements were on their way out, while four British devotees of the mixed hydromechanical system—Austin, Daimler, Jowett, and Riley—were about to adopt full hydraulics. Only Rolls-Royce would hold out, with their great faith in the old gearbox-driven servo, destined to see them into the era of disc brakes.

The last bastions of mechanical brakes were the stripped-specification sedans, Ford of Britain's 103E Popular (1953–59) and the standard Volkswagen, which did not acquire hydraulics until 1962. The custo-

Remembered as the first mass-produced car to feature alternating rather than direct-current electrics, the 1960 Plymouth Valiant (*below*) was also important as Chrysler Corporation's first compact, and as symbolizing the switch from the old long-stroke side-valve six (made with little change since the 1930s) to a new and modest overhead-valve unit mounted in the frame at a 30-degree slant. Styling was restrained, too, apart from the usual "dustbin lid" pressing on the trunk. Although 2.8 litres were not enough for any real performance, the automatic Valiant managed 90 mph (145 km/h) and an 0–50 mph (0–80 km/h) acceleration time of 12.6 seconds, roughly the potential of a full-sized American straight-eight in 1939. With a length of 184 in (4.7 m), the Valiant was still a large car by European standards. (*Opposite*) Kaiser-Frazer's Henry J sedan of 1951 was, by contrast, a modest package measuring 100 in (2.5 m) between wheel centres, and 166 in (4.2 m) between bumpers. Conceived as a farmer's car to follow in the wheel-tracks of the Model-A Ford, it was a conventional affair with coil-spring independent front suspension, semi-elliptics at the rear, open propeller shaft, and hypoid rear axle. Engines were plain side-valves bought from Kaiser's future partner, Willys-Overland: the Jeep's familiar 2.2-litre four and a 2.6-litre six. Styling was uninspired, and the first Henry Js had no external trunk access. Alas, the American public wanted more car, more output, and more acceleration, while fuel was still cheap and plentiful. It took nearly four years to sell 120,000 Henry Js. The Valiant managed close on 200,000 units in its first season alone.

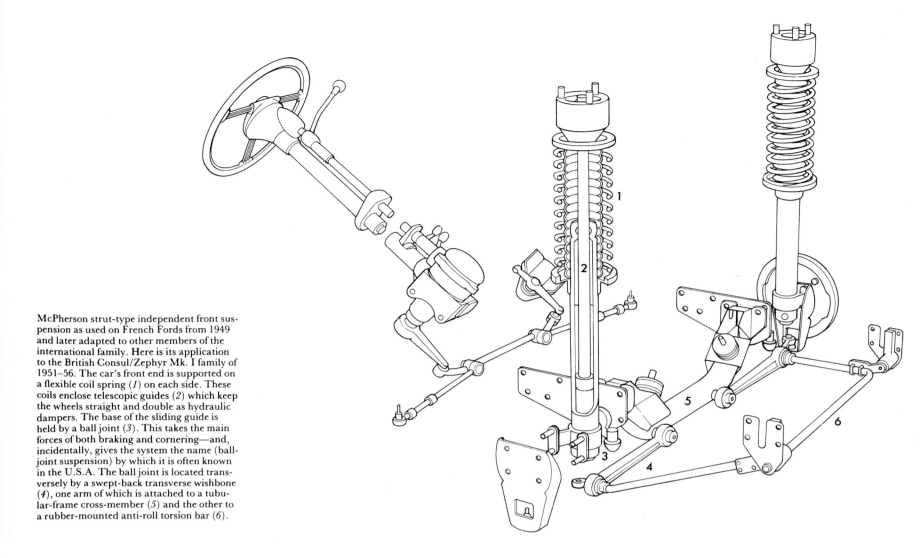

McPherson strut-type independent front suspension as used on French Fords from 1949 and later adapted to other members of the international family. Here is its application to the British Consul/Zephyr Mk. I family of 1951–56. The car's front end is supported on a flexible coil spring (*1*) on each side. These coils enclose telescopic guides (*2*) which keep the wheels straight and double as hydraulic dampers. The base of the sliding guide is held by a ball joint (*3*). This takes the main forces of both braking and cornering—and, incidentally, gives the system the name (ball-joint suspension) by which it is often known in the U.S.A. The ball joint is located transversely by a swept-back transverse wishbone (*4*), one arm of which is attached to a tubular-frame cross-member (*5*) and the other to a rubber-mounted anti-roll torsion bar (*6*).

mer who got a full-sized four-seater sedan for DM 4,000 (a bare 600 marks more than the 300-cc Goggomobil minicar cost) was unlikely to quibble over its crudities. Within a mere six years, however, he would be wanting to know why his "bargain" lacked disc brakes, and raising objections when he had to pay extra for them on such elderly designs as the basic Beetle and the Triumph Herald. While emergency braking systems remained largely unchanged, the deplorable plastic "umbrella" handle under the dash had almost had its day as well. Renault, who were content with one of these unpleasant devices on their otherwise excellent 16 (1965), returned to a floor mounting on their 12 in 1969, probably as a result of the safety drive. If one takes cars tested by the British motoring press as a fair measure, one may note that umbrella handles made up 45 % of the number in 1955, 40 % in 1960, and only 33 % in 1970. The foot-operated "handbrake" stayed an American preserve until Mercedes-Benz picked up the idea in 1968, although sudden-death devices working on the transmission had mercifully been dropped by both Fiat and Chrysler in the early sixties.

Anything made between 1951 and 1960, at all events, could be expected to have hydraulic drum brakes. Later examples were often less efficient than those of 1950–51, due to a new factor: decreasing wheel size. On sporting Classics of the early 1930s, brake-cooling problems had not existed, thanks to a 16-inch brake drum in a 19- or 20-inch wheel, especially since centre-lock wires were *de rigueur* in this class. But

wire wheels were dying out, replaced by the stronger and easier-to-clean disc, even on such traditional sporting machines as Alfa Romeo, Alvis, Bentley, Jaguar, Lagonda, and MG. The old order would return to favour, but not until 1956–57 when wires were a regular option on most British sports cars. Meanwhile, smaller wheels emerged, 16 in representing the standard European size in 1951. American cars then usually wore 15-in equipment, shrinking to 14 in by 1957 when the hairier V-8s were offering 300 horsepower or more—and some lesser models, still with V-8 options, were making do with 13 in four years later. By this time, 15 in was effectively the top limit in Europe, while the Mini, like the bubble-cars, wore tiny 10-in "boots". So there was less space for a brake drum and not enough for its cooling air. Drums heated up and expanded away from their shoes, just as linings lost their friction characteristics. Yet performance increased steadily: 75 mph (120 km/h) was now well within the compass of a stock 1.5-litre sedan, and a wide selection of 100-mph (160-km/h) sporting machinery was on sale. Thus, brake fade became a pressing problem.

The disc brake was the obvious answer. Essentially a development of the bicycle caliper brake, it had friction pads which moved axially to grip the sides of the disc. First fitted to Chrysler and Crosley cars in America as early as 1949–50, this method won prominence on Jaguar's competition sports models between 1952 and 1955. Pioneers of its application to touring models were Citroën (on the 1955 Déesse) with Jensen

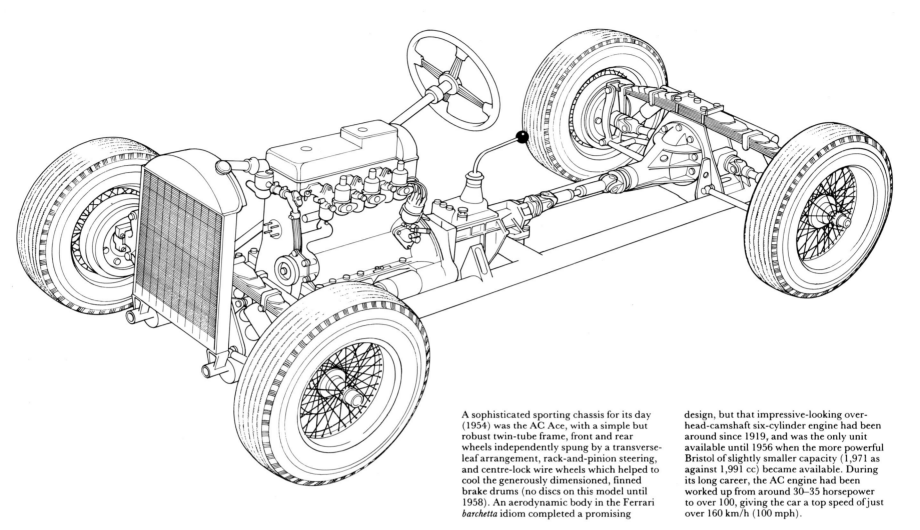

A sophisticated sporting chassis for its day (1954) was the AC Ace, with a simple but robust twin-tube frame, front and rear wheels independently spung by a transverse-leaf arrangement, rack-and-pinion steering, and centre-lock wire wheels which helped to cool the generously dimensioned, finned brake drums (no discs on this model until 1958). An aerodynamic body in the Ferrari *barchetta* idiom completed a promising design, but that impressive-looking over-head-camshaft six-cylinder engine had been around since 1919, and was the only unit available until 1956 when the more powerful Bristol of slightly smaller capacity (1,971 as against 1,991 cc) became available. During its long career, the AC engine had been worked up from around 30–35 horsepower to over 100, giving the car a top speed of just over 160 km/h (100 mph).

and Triumph a year later, although these firms—like most other initial supporters of the system—used discs only at the front. By contrast, Jaguar, whose XK150 (1957) was the next convert, insisted on a four-wheel installation and never offered anything else. A good proportion of the world's specialist manufacturers had taken the plunge by 1960 and, three years later, 24 makers listed front discs as either standard or optional equipment. All-disc layouts were found on Ferrari, Iso, Jaguar, Jensen, Lotus, Maserati, Mercedes-Benz, and Porsche. Fiat and Simca offered them only on sports models, but significant recruits in the family-car sector were Lancia and Renault. Even more interesting was the absence of any American brand except Studebaker, who fitted them to the sadly abortive Avanti sports coupé (1962).

American makers, too, were beginning to list front-disc options by 1966. Few European factories now relied on drums alone, and none of these made anything bigger than a 1,200-cc model. Alfa Romeo and Rolls-Royce had joined the all-disc brigade. At the end of our period, no quality machine (save the huge, ceremonial Phantom VI Rolls-Royce) lacked front discs, while Cadillac and Lincoln had standardized them in America. All but the smallest Fiats and Renaults wore them at the rear as well. In regard to brake actuation, dual master cylinders had long been a regular adjunct of hydraulic brakes, being seen on the big six-cylinder Fiats as far back as 1931. Safety, during our period, called for split-circuit systems with tandem master cylinders, isolating one

pair of brakes from the other. These gained serious currency from 1966 onward, being general practice in America by 1969, and were also found on Alfa Romeo, BMW, Citroën, the latest European Fords, Lancia, Saab, and Volvo.

Keeping brakes cool and fade-proof was not enough. Servos were again engaging the attention of designers. They had long been used, the gearbox-drive Hispano-Suiza system (employed by Rolls-Royce) since 1919, and the Belgian Dewandre *servofrein à dépression* since 1923. The latter was applied to several popular makes, including Citroën and Hillman, in the 1920s, but was subsequently cast aside on the usual grounds of cost, not to mention the greater efficiency and modest pedal pressures resulting from the general adoption of hydraulics. By the outbreak of World War II, it had again become the preserve of luxury and sporting machines. More speed, however, calls for more braking effort. The driver of a Cadillac or Rolls-Royce was always in need of some assistance, and so might be the owners of 2-litre family sedans in an era when these were capable of 95 mph (150 km/h). Thus, vacuum servos came back into the picture during the 1960s. Citroën, predictably, preferred hydraulic pressure built up by the same engine-drive pump that supported their Déesse—as we shall see—and, in addition, furnished servo assistance to the clutch and gear change.

Servos were standard by 1960 on the heavier and more expensive American cars—not just Cadillacs, Lincolns, and Imperials, but also

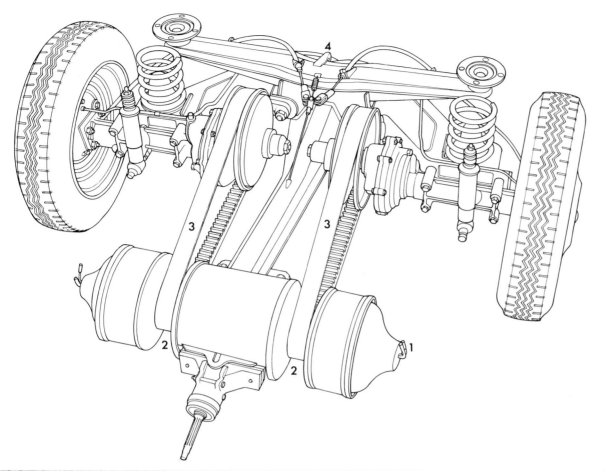

(*Top left*) Simplest of the automatics, DAF's Variomatic Drive, as used by this Dutch manufacturer from 1958 onwards. The drive was transmitted to a transverse countershaft (1) with the inboard halves of two vee pulleys (2) attached to it. The power was then taken by two belts (3), each driving a separate rear wheel. Movement of the pulleys altered the gearing by changing their effective diameter, while a reduction in manifold suction would widen the gaps between the flanges to lower the ratio. The transmission was entirely stepless, and free from the "hunting" of a normal automatic. The whole rear end is mounted on a separate sub-frame (4).

(*Bottom left*) Compact at 142 in (3.6 m) long, frugal at 40 mpg (6.5 litres/100 km), and innocent of frills, the 1964 DAF sedan gave no clues to its ingenious and painless Variomatic transmission. All-independent suspension and rack-and-pinion steering were to be expected on a small family sedan born in 1958. And if air-cooled flat-twins sounded a trifle barbaric in the age of the Mini—well, other respected users included BMW, Citroën, and Panhard, the last being a veteran with 73 years of car-making behind it. The DAF's 62 mph (100 km/h) were quite enough, since braking was not its strong suit, while 0–50 mph (0–80 km/h) took 22 seconds, or nearly as long as it took a standard Mini to reach 60 mph (100 km/h). But with only 746 cc under that short bonnet, there's a price to pay for not having to shift gears at any time.

(*Opposite, top*) Triumph switched to fuel-injected engines on their TR5 sports car of 1967, which combined the body and independent rear suspension of the superseded TR4A with a new 2.5-litre six-cylinder engine descended from the 1961 Standard Vanguard Six. Top speed went up from the old four's 109 mph (175 km/h) to around 120 mph (192 km/h). To meet American emission standards, there was a twin-carburettor six as well, the TR250. The interesting Surrey top—available either in metal or as a light frame with hooding—was an option on TR4s and TR5s, which anticipated Porsche's better-known Targa semi-convertible of 1967.

(*Opposite, bottom*) Power assistance for most things on a fine 1968 Euro-American from Jensen, who had built a luxury sedan with a Ford V-8 motor as long ago as 1936. This Vignale-styled Interceptor featured a 6.3-litre V-8 Chrysler engine, a three-speed automatic gearbox, dual-circuit power disc brakes with tandem master cylinders, power-operated windows, and heated rear window. Power steering would not, however, be part of the package until the 1970 season. Interestingly, too, Jensen, who had fitted glass-fibre bodies to sedans in the 1954–66 period, now reverted to all-steel construction. £3,742 was a lot of money to pay for a car in the late sixties, though 13 mpg (22 litres/100 km) was less of a worry while fuel was still cheap and plentiful. And a quiet 120 mph (196 km/h) appealed to nearly 4,500 customers between 1967 and 1973.

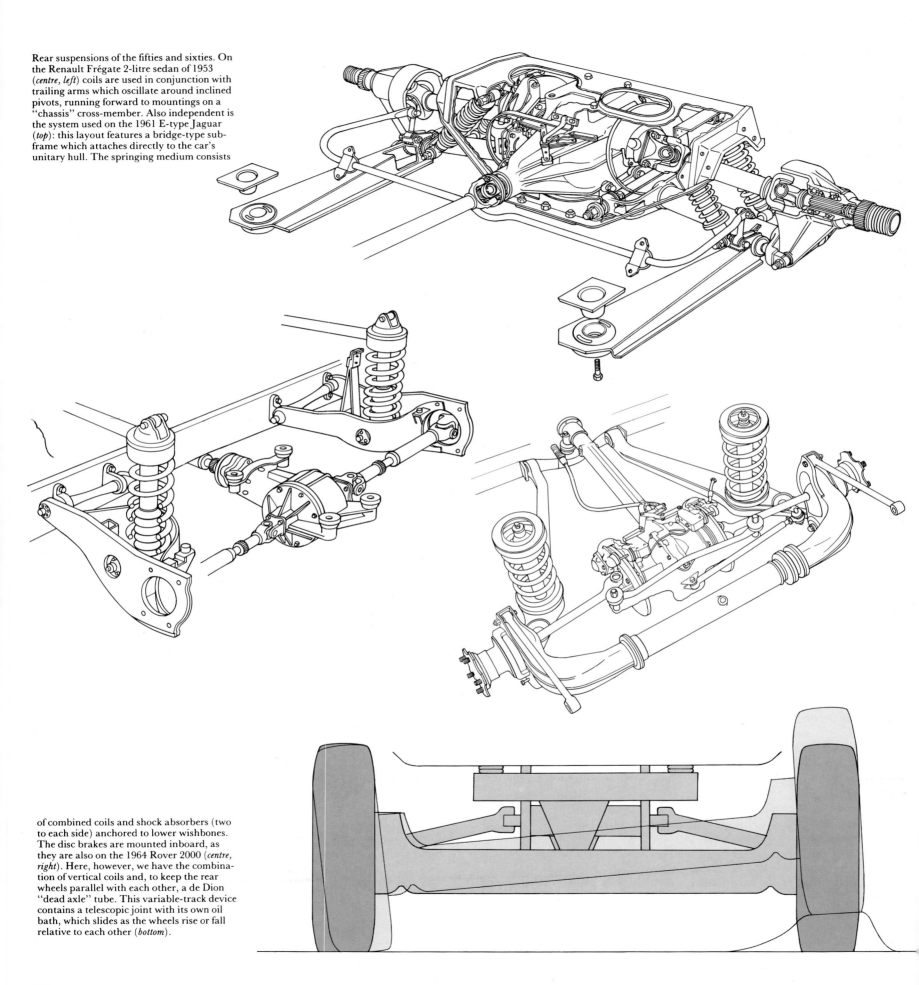

Rear suspensions of the fifties and sixties. On the Renault Frégate 2-litre sedan of 1953 (*centre, left*) coils are used in conjunction with trailing arms which oscillate around inclined pivots, running forward to mountings on a "chassis" cross-member. Also independent is the system used on the 1961 E-type Jaguar (*top*): this layout features a bridge-type sub-frame which attaches directly to the car's unitary hull. The springing medium consists

of combined coils and shock absorbers (two to each side) anchored to lower wishbones. The disc brakes are mounted inboard, as they are also on the 1964 Rover 2000 (*centre, right*). Here, however, we have the combination of vertical coils and, to keep the rear wheels parallel with each other, a de Dion "dead axle" tube. This variable-track device contains a telescopic joint with its own oil bath, which slides as the wheels rise or fall relative to each other (*bottom*).

the bigger Buicks and Ford's prestigious Thunderbird. Anything in the 120-mph (195-km/h) class demanded power assistance, too, as did such family machinery as Humbers, Datsuns, Mercedes-Benz, and Rovers. The next step was inevitable: small cars would need help as well. These were getting bigger, heavier, and faster. The 1951 Hillman Minx was 157 in (4.02 m) long, weighed 2,072 lb (945 kg), and could reach 70 mph (112 km/h). Its 1968 counterpart was only 11 in (28 cm) longer, but engine development enabled a mere 230 cc of extra capacity to deliver nearly double the output, plus a 15-mph (22-km/h) increase in top speed. The brakes were now too heavy in relation to performance, so a servo was added to the options list. Similar assistance was given to parallel models like the 124 Fiat, the Audi, and the Peugeot 403.

While wheel sizes went down, tyres were undergoing a major evolution. At the beginning of our period, speeds of around 125 mph (200 km/h) were within the compass of Jaguars, Ferraris, and Aston Martins, yet there were no tyres that could cope with such performance. The tubeless type, available in America by 1948, and in Europe some five years later, was a step towards simplicity but, in itself, contributed nothing to the need for better adhesion. During the 1950s, though, the radial-ply tyre started to make headway. This replaced the earlier cross-ply type, in which alternate layers of reinforcing cords are used at 45 degrees to the centre plane. On the new type, the cords run radially to the tyre, from one bead to another, while additional bracing plies—of steel cord on the Michelin version—were set under the tread. The result was a tyre of greater vertical flexibility, superior rolling resistance, better grip, and longer life. These virtues were won at the cost of a harsher ride and a higher noise level. It is also true to say that a radial induces a larger amount of breakaway when the latter occurs: still, the cornering speed limit is far higher than on a cross-ply. Radials were regular equipment on all high-performance cars by the end of our second decade, while even on family sedans a majority of motorists were specifying them.

Supporting the vehicle on a beam axle at each end was now virtually reserved for all-terrain models like the Jeep, Landrover, and Toyota Land Cruiser. We may pass quickly by such eccentricities as the early Bond Minicar, a three-wheeler on which "suspension" was limited to fat tyres and tiny wheels, albeit only at the back. Independent front suspensions in general use were the coil-and-wishbone type, usually with short and long arms that dispensed with the uncouth "curtseying" of 1930s versions; the transverse-leaf arrangement, where the springs are coupled to swivelling axles; and torsion bars, rigidly coupled to the lower wishbone at its chassis pivot and to a fixed point down the chassis length, a system favoured by Chrysler, Jaguar, Morris, and Volkswagen among others.

A variation on the coil-spring layout was the McPherson strut suspension, which used vertical coils and rigid stub axles. It was taken up by Ford for their French range in 1948, reaching the British models in 1951 and the German cars in 1952, although it would not attain a really wide currency until the 1970s. In the meantime, honours were generally divided between the traditional coil system and torsion bars. Longitudinal semi-elliptics at the rear remained common practice throughout our period, being still used on such makes as Chrysler, Datsun, Ford, Hillman, Oldsmobile, and Rambler even in 1969. The combination of a rigid axle and coils—as on some General Motors cars and on Volvos—called for a locating rod if the handling was not to suffer disastrously. On some cars with front-wheel drive, dead rear axles were supported by transverse torsion bars (the original Citroën traction, Audi) or by a rigid axle with transverse leaf spring (DKW).

True independent systems took a while to reach general acceptance but, of the German makers, Mercedes-Benz, Porsche, Volkswagen, and

Borgward used nothing else after the war. The swing axles and coils favoured by Mercedes-Benz and Triumph could create appreciable "hopping" in tight bends. A combination of coils and trailing arms was preferred by BMW, Chevrolet (on the Corvette), Fiat, Renault, and Hillman on the Imp. Volkswagen stayed with their swinging half-axles and transverse torsion bars. Lotus, on the 1957 Elite, adapted the McPherson strut arrangement to the back end. On their earlier sports models (1954), AC used the same transverse leaf and wishbone arrangement at both ends, but they discarded it in favour of coils when installing Ford's high-performance V-8s in the final Cobra series. Also converted to independent rear suspension (in 1961) were Jaguar, who mounted their whole assembly, including the inboard disc brakes, on a detachable bridge-piece. In this case, the actual suspension medium consisted of twin coil springs on each side, the wheels being located by parallel transverse links of unequal and longitudinal radius arms.

Ingenious, too, was the system applied to BMC Minis from 1959 onward, with rubber cones in torsion as the springing medium. This arrangement gave a variable rate, yet needed no lubrication. It would lead to the Hydrolastic interconnected springs found on the 1100 model in 1962, as well as on subsequent 1800s, with application to Minis after 1964. Here, interconnection was obtained by feeding hydraulic pipes into the cones, and the water-based hydraulic system ran down the sides of the car, incorporating the dampers. Not that it was the first such arrangement: on the 2CV Citroën, the simplest of self-levelling systems had been used. Leading arms and horizontal coils at the front were connected with trailing arms and another set of horizontal coils at the rear. This worked admirably, although the alarming roll angles caused by fast cornering would never have been acceptable on any vehicle of real performance. In its original 375-cc form, after all, the 2CV was capable of merely 40 mph (65 km/h).

Citroën soon passed on to better things. Their hydropneumatic suspension was first seen at the back of the old 15/6 in 1954. Two years later, it had been engineered into the remarkable Déesse. The car itself was a sensation, with shark-nose shape, plastic roof, "wheel at each corner" layout, and inboard front disc brakes. But the springing was a real *tour de force*, consisting basically of four oleo-pneumatic struts, with gas compression replacing the metal springs. The system was controlled by Lockheed brake fluid, metered through a regulator driven off the engine by a pump. This adjusted the height of the car from the ground, as well as providing power for jacking in the event of a puncture. Nor was the suspension the pump's sole responsibility. The hydropneumatics also lent assistance to the clutch, gear-change, brakes, steering, and gearbox—although the transmission was not an automatic, and no automatic member of the D family would be listed during our period. *The Motor* called it "the most complicated car made anywhere" and, perhaps wisely, Citroën soon backed the original DS19 with a simplified ID, on which hydraulic aids were confined to the springing. Yet it was certainly the most sophisticated car of the period, and only a sudden humpback bridge could catch it unawares.

Packard's contemporary self-levelling system used 9-ft (2.75-m) torsion bars running down the chassis, wound up anticlockwise to the front and clockwise to the rear, an electric motor being used to adjust the trim. It worked well but, by this time, Studebaker-Packard were in grave financial trouble, and the senior make was doomed to a speedy decline into a badge-engineered Studebaker, on which such devices would have been superfluous. Armstrong Selectaride electrically controlled rear shock absorbers with four settings, available in Britain by 1962, were taken up by Facel Vega, Gordon-Keeble, and Humber for their prestige Imperial sedan.

Air suspensions were tried by Cadillac in 1958, Borgward in 1960,

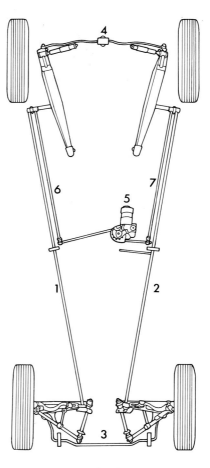

(*Top left*) There is no immediate indication that Cadillac's 1957 Eldorado Brougham is fitted with air suspension: it does not "squat" on its haunches when stationary with the engine switched off. But the new-fangled medium was leak-prone, and disappointing sales—704 in two seasons—highlighted the common American preference for the safe and known way of doing things. For his $13,000-odd, of course, the customer got a lot more than just a 6-litre 335-horsepower V-8 engine, automatic, and power steering. Inclusive were air conditioning, separate front and rear heater units, radio, a six-way front power seat with built-in memory, power door locks, power trunk lid, tinted glass, a brushed stainless-steel roof, four horns, and such dainty touches as a full vanity case (with six magnetized silver tumblers, lipstick, and stick cologne), and a perfume atomizer (by Arpège) in the rear-seat armrest. On this model 45 different interior colour/trim combinations were offered.

(*Top right*) Befitting an American luxury car was the sophisticated Torsion-Level inter-linked suspension system used on 1955–56 Packards. Its basis was (*1, 2*) a pair of torsion bars, 2.75 m (108 in) long, running the length of the chassis and attached to both suspensions with stabilizers (*3, 4*) at each end. To allow for changes of load, an electric motor (*5*) was coupled to a pair of shorter auxiliary torsion bars (*6, 7*). This motor cut in if the rear of the car was either higher or lower than its standard position, while a 5-second time lag ensured that the auxiliary system would not operate merely for a bump in the road.

(*Bottom*) Citroën's hydropneumatic suspension in its simplest form, as applied only to the rear of the traditional 15CV six-cylinder for 1954: later models used the hydropneumatics all round. Hydraulic pressure derives from a pump driven off the engine crankshaft (*1*) and supplied from a firewall-mounted reservoir (*2*). The fluid is delivered to a hydropneumatic accumulator (*3*) with a distributor valve which pressurizes the system when the pump is not working. With the pump in operation, the valve feeds the fluid under pressure to recharge the accumulator and feed the suspension system. The circuit passes to an automatic height corrector (*4*), from which single pipes run to each hydropneumatic spring unit (*5*), these being gas-filled spheres screwed to the end of the suspension cylinder. An isolation cock (*6*), between accumulator and height corrector, allows isolation of the front part of the circuit from the rear, thus locking the suspension at static height when the engine is turned off. This cock is reopened automatically by the first depression of the clutch pedal. In the car's boot is a manual override (*7*) to the height corrector, used to assist with wheel changes.

(*Right*) A shark shape—but not a predatory car. Citroën's Déesse wasn't noted for sheer straight-line speed or for fearsome acceleration. The top-of-the-range cabriolet has, of course, all the hydropneumatic aids to painless driving as well as the ingenious suspension. It was made in modest numbers from 1961 to 1971, Henri Chapron (famed for his superb pre-war coachwork on Delage chassis) doing the conversion. The car looks at its best with the top down: in closed form, the absence of rear quarter windows give it a heavy appearance as well as negligible rearward vision. This 1964 model retains the aged long-stroke 1,911-cc four-cylinder engine of a basic type used since 1934/35.

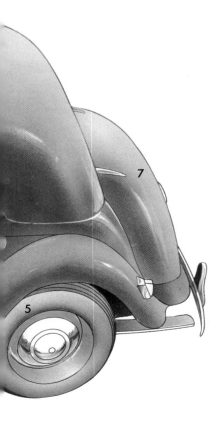

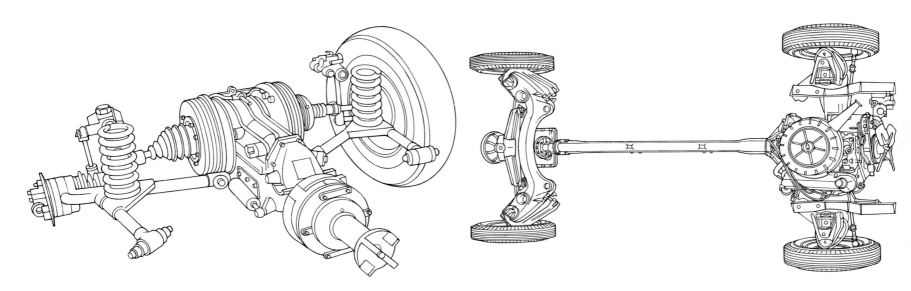

(*Above*) Transaxles. The V-6 Lancia Aurelia of 1950–58 (*left*) always wore its four-speed gearbox on the rear axle. This is the early version with fully independent rear springing by vertical coils which are located by diagonal swinging arms. Note also the mounting of the brakes inboard on the final drive assembly, which made for complicated maintenance. On the 1961 Pontiac Tempest (*right*), a transaxle was once again used, possibly because it shared its essential unitary structure with the rear-engined Chevrolet Corvair, and—like the Corvair—it featured swing-axle independent rear suspension. The Pontiac's oddest feature was, however, a curved flexible drive-shaft, said to damp out some of the vibration inherent in a big four-cylinder engine, in effect half of one of the Division's existing V-8 designs.

(*Below*) Power steering, as standard equipment fitted to the 1968 NSU Ro80 sedan with front-wheel drive and a Wankel-type engine. For safety, the steering box (*1*) is mounted high up on the firewall: the steering gear itself is of rack-and-pinion type. Power assistance is furnished by a vane-type pump (*2*) driven off the engine by two vee belts, and fed with hydraulic fluid from a tank (*3*). Thence it is delivered under pressure to a servo valve (*4*) adjacent to the steering box, and brought into action by movement of the steering wheel to left or right.

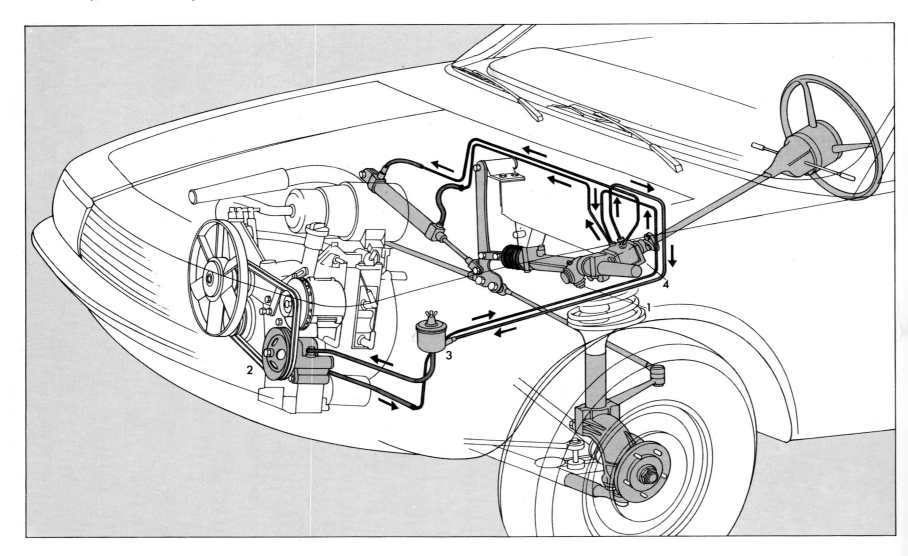

and Mercedes-Benz in 1963. Engine-driven compressors powered all these systems, although in the last case they were supplementary to the standard suspension—by coils and wishbones at the front, and by swing axles at the rear. The Cadillac used a rubber air dome at each corner, and no conventional springs whatever. This car, like the Citroën Ds, leapt into action with an obbligato of reproachful moans, but the main problem was that the system leaked. The Mercedes-Benz arrangements were simply too expensive in terms of the improvement they gave, though they survived on the ultra-costly 6.3-litre 600 limousine until it was finally withdrawn from production in 1981, and they were applied to some of the more expensive owner-driven sedans. The six-cylinder Borgward's two-year run was terminated by the maker's bankruptcy in 1961: few were made, and fewer still with the air springs. Perhaps significantly, when production was resumed briefly in Mexico in 1967, no mention was made of any suspension other than the orthodox type.

On cars with rear-wheel drive, the hypoid bevel reigned supreme. But on a number of models, notably Lancia and the Pontiac Tempest of 1962, there was a reversion to the transaxle, in which the gearbox was combined with the differential. While this helped to give a more even weight distribution, and was adopted by its American advocates for better front-seat legroom, it posed problems of maintenance and was never widely employed. A more lasting development was the limited-slip differential, which prevents wheel-spin when accelerating away from a standstill. This was a valuable adjunct by the early 1960s, since many back ends were being made to transmit 300 horsepower or more. As early as 1951, it was standard equipment on the Spanish Pegaso sports car. By the end of our period, it was found on such rapid machinery as the Euro-American AC, Iso, and Jensen, all Ferraris and Lamborghinis, the E-type Jaguar, and the V-8 Morgan. It was also an option on the six-cylinder sedans made by BMW, Jaguar, and Mercedes-Benz. Meanwhile, the de Dion rear axle, a curved dead tube which carried the weight of the car but did not transmit the drive, reappeared on various models: notably Allard, Aston Martin, Frazer Nash, and Pegaso in the 1950s, besides the Rover 2000 of 1964 in conjunction with coil springs. On the Rover, it was selected to furnish a combination of good handling and low unsprung weight. It was never, though, widely used except on racing cars.

Power-assisted steering was more controversial than automatic transmission, largely because it took all the feel out of directing a car. In its more extreme forms, it gave the driver an impression that he was assisting the car, rather than the opposite. However, it was a necessary development in the U.S.A., where cars were growing in weight and bulk. There was also a limitation on the gearing-down which increased the number of steering-wheel turns from lock to lock. Five and a half turns were becoming the norm in America, but even the three and a half turns required by an average European 1.5-litre sedan felt undergeared by the standards of Vintage cars.

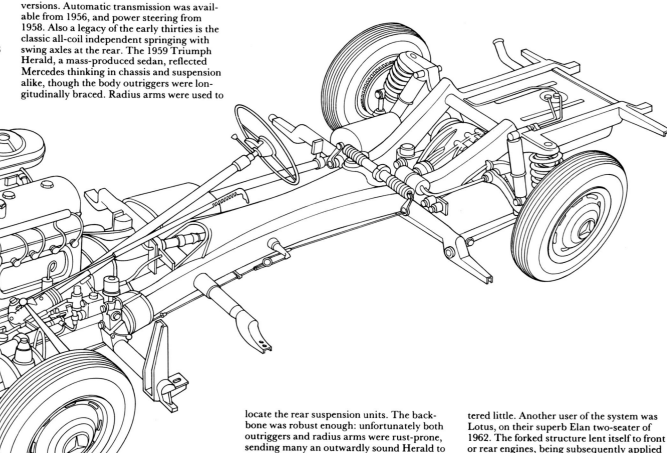

Backbone frames. Shown here is the classic Mercedes-Benz construction inherited from pre-war and still used on the big 300 sedans of 1951–62, though smaller models would switch to true unitary construction from 1953 onwards. This model featured a 3-litre single overhead-camshaft six-cylinder engine developing 115 horsepower, but higher outputs were extracted from later fuel-injected versions. Automatic transmission was available from 1956, and power steering from 1958. Also a legacy of the early thirties is the classic all-coil independent springing with swing axles at the rear. The 1959 Triumph Herald, a mass-produced sedan, reflected Mercedes thinking in chassis and suspension alike, though the body outriggers were longitudinally braced. Radius arms were used to locate the rear suspension units. The backbone was robust enough: unfortunately both outriggers and radius arms were rust-prone, sending many an outwardly sound Herald to the wrecking yard. The same backbone was applied to a sports-car derivative, the Spitfire (*photo page 199*), the idea being an entirely logical one for sporting machines on which any intrusion into the cockpit centre mattered little. Another user of the system was Lotus, on their superb Elan two-seater of 1962. The forked structure lent itself to front or rear engines, being subsequently applied to the Europa coupé with mid-mounted Renault unit (*photo page 51*). The Elan had all-independent strut-type suspension, a powerful twin overhead-camshaft four-cylinder Lotus-Ford engine, and all-disc brakes.

Cadillac and Chrysler were first in 1951 with a hydraulic system connected in parallel to the track rod, between the chassis and the steering arm. These principles were followed by all subsequent arrangements, although Citroën naturally linked the steering gear to their complex hydropneumatic circuit and Studebaker briefly tried a mechanical device driven off the crankshaft by a pulley. By 1953, the entire U.S. industry was offering this new form of assistance. It came on 93 % of all new Cadillacs and, even in the middle-class sector, 45 % of Chrysler customers and 40 % of Oldsmobile's had tired of sawing away at the steering-wheel. A year later, Cadillac fitted it as standard, while it remained an extra on Imperials until 1955 and on Lincolns until 1956. Nominally, it was still an extra on lesser breeds of American automobiles in 1969, but only 16 % of customers were content to do without it. Apparently, too, the sportier American motorist wanted acceleration, "performance packs", and illicit straight-line speed rather than precise handling, since 66 % of that year's Ford Mustangs were power-steered.

In Europe, Citroën led off during 1955, followed by Rolls-Royce, Bentley, Facel Vega, and the usual procession of up-market manufacturers: Armstrong Siddeley, Mercedes-Benz, and Jaguar. After this, it was the usual procession of semi-prestige sedans, with Rover in 1960, BMC in 1962, Opel in 1964, and Vauxhall in 1965. BMW's move back to six cylinders in 1968 brought them into the power-steering league as well. Assistance could also be had on super-cars in the Aston Martin/ Ferrari bracket, although normally as an optional extra.

The rack-and-pinion steering gear made great strides, yet it would not become nearly universal until the middle seventies. Always noted for its direct and positive action, it was quite widely used in the first decade of our century, but was discarded because of the backlash it transmitted to the steering-wheel. Intriguingly, it was an adjunct of one

Safety measures. This Alfa Romeo collapsible steering column dates from 1975, but typifies progress already apparent in the late sixties. Much promoted as a safe vehicle, the 1964 Rover 2000 (below) was built round a steel cage with a bulkhead strong enough to prevent the engine's working its way back into the passenger compartment in a collision: the skeleton version was drivable, with alarming-looking tubes on the rear quarter panel, namely the petrol-tank breathers.

This diagrammatic view of the Rover's 3.5-litre automatic-transmission development (1969) shows some of the features singled out by the makers as "safety equipment": (1) resilient padding for the interior quarters, (2) front-seat belt anchorages (they were also furnished at the rear), (3) child-proof rear door locks, (4) softly padded sun visors, (5) switches "differing in shape, feel, and movement" to avoid pulling the wrong button, (6) heater air intake above the level of other vehicles' exhausts, (7) high-mounted steering box in a position where it cannot push the wheel and column up in an accident, (8) dished steering wheel, and (9) fuel tank mounted within the main structure and insulated from the passengers by a steel bulkhead. Also on the "safety" list was the linear speedometer, although a good few owners of the model (including the present writer) would regard this as a questionable asset.

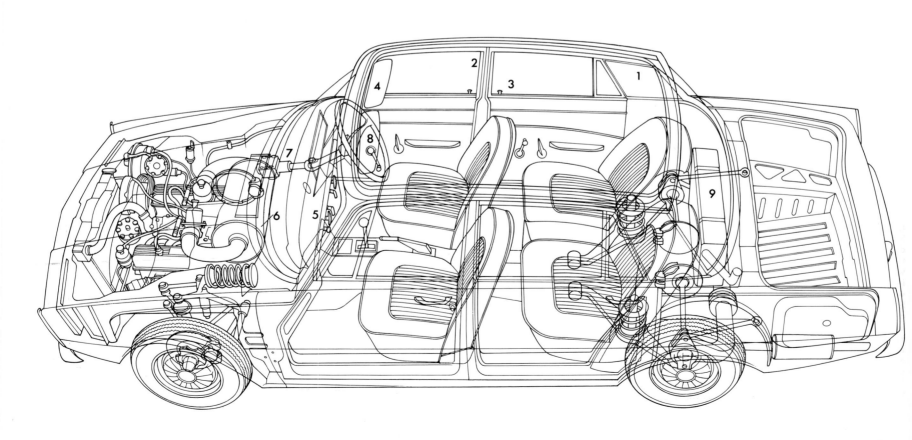

of the first successful independent front-suspension systems, that of Maurice Sizaire in 1905. In its modern form, the racks were damped by spring-loaded metal or plastic inserts pressing on their backs. Already in the 1930s, it had been successfully applied to the cars with front-wheel drive by Citroën, DKW, and Adler. By the late 1940s, it was found on two members of the new post-war generation, ·the Morris Minor and the Peugeot 203. The Saab had it from the start in 1949, as might be expected from the Swedish car's DKW ancestry. Jaguar, who had tried it on their competition models, applied the system to the touring line as well in 1955. Outside America, the industry was quick to spot its advantages. The first cars from DAF and a revived NSU·company came out with such equipment in 1958, Mazda and Triumph being among 1959's recruits. Others fitting rack-and-pinion systems in the 1960s included Hillman, Opel, Porsche, and Vauxhall, joined at the very end of our period by Ford of Europe and Fiat.

The chassis frame was by no means dead. Although Americans preferred perimeter types to the old cruciforms, they still regarded unitary construction as a tiresome question-mark. Two of Ford's more expensive cars, the Thunderbird and the Lincoln, dispensed with separate chassis in 1959, but both were back with this older layout by 1969. Backbones were used by Volkswagen, Porsche, and Skoda, as well as by Mercedes-Benz on their pre-war "hangover" types. Triumph returned to traditional methods in 1959 by building the Herald on a double-backbone basis, which was said (correctly) to be stronger and (less correctly) to be rustproof. Except for Mercedes-Benz, Jaguar, and (from 1966) Rolls-Royce, the specialist makers tended to stay with separate frames long after the demise of a custom-body industry that cloaked the cars individually.

But otherwise the separate chassis was losing its grip. Austin quit in 1954, Standard in 1955, and Rootes in 1956, while on the Continent all post-1952 Fiats were unitary structures. Volvo reserved the old arrangements for their antiquated and ponderous PV800, a hangover from the 1930s which catered for the Swedish taxi trade and for chauffeur-driven executives until 1959. Unitary construction itself pursued the principles laid down at the time of its inception in the 1930s, although the Citroën/Fiat concept of a "wheelbarrow"—to carry the mechanical elements—was taken a step further on the Rover 2000 of 1964. This model was welded into a complete skeleton including the outlines of roof, bonnet, and boot, then was dressed with its mechanical elements and outer skin.

Tubular space frames· were used to considerable effect on specialist competition cars, although fitting the machinery—or, for that matter, the crew—into the resultant structure was something of a problem. On 1954's Mercedes-Benz, a low profile was achieved by tilting the engine at 45 degrees, and this rendered a right-hand-drive option impossible, though it did not require the use of fuel injection instead of carburettors. A glance at the jungle of small-diameter tubing that made up the 1961 "Birdcage" Maserati was a clear indication of its unsuitability for all but racing, despite its undoubtedly optimum combination of strength and lightness.

We shall encounter glass-fibre techniques in detail when discussing bodies. Suffice it to say that the material was first adapted to car bodies in California in 1950, and initially applied to a series-production automobile on 1953's Chevrolet Corvette sports roadster. By 1956, however, Berkeley had built a small sports model around three sections of bolted-up glass fibre and an aluminium bulkhead, while Colin Chapman's Lotus Elite came a year afterward. The latter was constructed from three major mouldings bonded together, with only three important

(*Right*) What looks right is right—nearly 330,000 discriminating customers in a short decade can't be wrong. The shape suggests the Citroën Déesse, and Rover's 2000 of 1964 was nearly as awkward to work on. But even in 90-horsepower single-carburettor form with four-speed manual transmission, the 2-litre overhead-camshaft engine propelled the car at 105 mph (168 km/h), motorway cruising speed was a comfortable 90 mph (145 km/h), and with gentle driving one could average 31 mpg (9 litres/100 km). One was, of course, always conscious that the 2000 was a four: customers had to wait until 1968 for a V-8 alternative, and even then automatic was compulsory until 1972.

metal components—the front suspension frame, bonded-in mountings for the other mechanical elements, and the windscreen hoop which had built-in jacking points and supports for the door hinges. The final drive unit bolted directly at the rear onto the bottom moulding, with no structural problems at all. True, early shells did not line up very happily, and the finish of mouldings left much to be desired. But the Elite's misfortunes were not born of its avant-garde structure: rather, they were a result of the maker's lack of experience with series production. Lotus chose a separate backbone chassis for their next car, because it was intended to have an open body and would therefore lack the reinforcement conferred by the Elite's fixed roof.

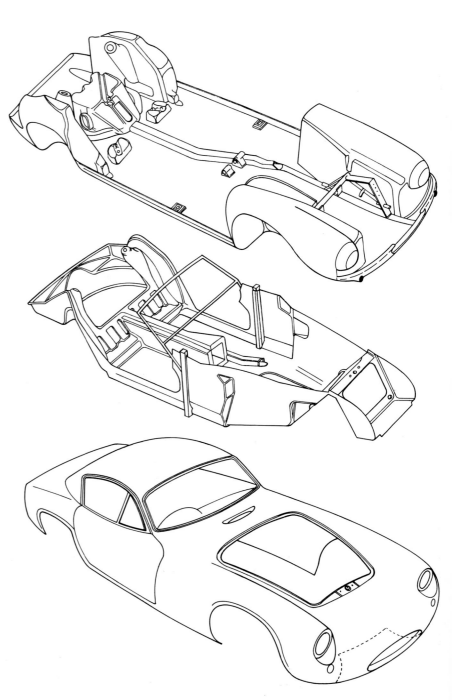

The marriage of glass-fibre and unitary construction, on the Lotus Elite sports coupé (1958). The whole structure is built up in three main mouldings. These consist of (*top*) the undertray with wheel wells, a front sub-frame to take the suspension units, and the differential mounting; (*centre*) the interior chassis/body panels, transmission tunnel, and engine bay; (*bottom*) the upper body with roof and wings. Doors, bonnet, and boot lid were separate mouldings, and the only metal elements were the front sub-frame and the tubular windscreen hoop.

3

BODIES
– BEAUTIFUL AND OTHERWISE

The stylist had integrated the motor car long before it became truly unitary in construction. Radiators had vanished behind grilles, dumb-irons were casualties of independent suspension, spare wheels had been tidied into boots, and lamps merged into grilles or fenders. The greatest stylistic influence at the beginning of the 1950s, the Cadillac Sixty Special of 1938, retained a separate chassis frame, and so did the Cadillacs of 1969. Yet nobody, except the public-relations people, referred to these as Cadillacs with bodies by the Fisher or Fleetwood Divisions of General Motors Corporation. At a more exotic level, only students of the body beautiful were really concerned whether a Ferrari was clothed by Bertone, Pininfarina, or Scaglietti: it was a Ferrari. While almost every car out of Maranello in 1951 had been a one-off, such extravaganzas, when encountered, were no more than styling prototypes for the future. The rear-engined Berlinetta Boxer flat-twelve would not go on sale until 1973, and thus is outside our period of reference. However, visitors to the 1968 Turin Show were given a preview of its appearance, if not its mechanics, in the non-running P6 coupé displayed by Pininfarina.

As we have seen, the specialist car manufacturer was slower to commit himself to unitary construction. Alfa Romeo had taken the plunge in 1950, Mercedes-Benz in 1953, Jaguar in 1956, and Rolls-Royce ten years later. But Ferrari and Jensen still built on chassis frames, as did Triumph and Morgan at a lower level. Still, whereas in 1939—and even to a lesser extent in 1950—there had been Saoutchik Delahayes and Hooper Rolls-Royce (though not, alas, Le Baron Lincolns), the decline would end in death after a decade. Of eleven purveyors of *haute couture* who exhibited at London's Earls Court in 1951, only five survived into 1961. With the demise of James Young in 1967, the great British "coachbuilt" tradition came to a close.

During our period, the German custom-body industry was effectively reduced to the supply of limited-series cabriolets for the big battalions. In France, the house of Figoni ceased operations in 1955 with a small series of Simca convertibles, there being no more Delages or Delahayes on which to exercise their craft. Chapron's decline was even more poignant. A special 15CV Citroën limousine—built for the President of the Republic, no less, in 1955—incorporated assorted hardware from French Fords, Chevrolet stop-lights, Bentley door handles, and a 1949 Buick rear window! The demand for "specials" on more mundane chassis was fading away: Plymouth shipped 20,762 cars without bodies between 1930 and 1942, but only 10,645 in the more prosperous years from 1951 to 1955. As for Cadillac, the 1938–50 chassis shipments, apart from specially lengthened "commercials" for ambulance and

hearse builders, amounted to 128 units. Thereafter only 44 were delivered, the last of these in 1963.

Not all was gloom. There was the shining exception of Italy. Before the war, connoisseurs of the exotic went to Paris or London according to taste, with an occasional glance at Berlin or Brussels—Belgian coachbuilders outlived the nation's chassis-makers by several years—but now they flocked to Turin. We shall meet the actual work of the Italians in a later chapter: let us note for the moment that they either devoted themselves to the creation of inspired shapes for volume production, like Bertone's Alfa Romeo Giulietta coupé (1954), or quietly transformed themselves into car builders in their own right, just as William Lyons of Swallow Coachbuilding had done in the 1930s with his SS and later with Jaguar. The line of demarcation was narrow, and sometimes a maker backtracked. Moretti, for instance, switched at the end of the 1950s from costly and none-too-successful twin overhead-camshaft miniatures, to Fiat derivatives which were not obviously Fiats.

Styling was sometimes subordinated to engineering. Arguably, with elaborate testing programmes extending from the Arctic Circle to the Sahara, it was becoming ever more difficult to produce a bad car. Mistakes, when they happened, were the result of poor market research or, alternatively, of premature release which reduced the customer to an unwilling member of the experimental department.

Disasters were nevertheless possible. At Chrysler in the early fifties, a constant battle was waged between the stylists and Corporation president Kaufman T. Keller, who dismissed the shapes of GM and Ford products as "jello-mold" and insisted that car boots should be able to carry a milk-churn in the vertical position. Hence, a style just about acceptable in 1950 had run its course by 1953, losing Plymouth two places in the sales-race list and, worse still, a quarter of a million sales in one year. The necessary and overdue reaction, masterminded by stylist Virgil Exner, went too far. Tail fins could be forgiven in 1957, when everyone else was adding them, but the abominable "dustbin lids" of 1957–61 could not.

Also to be laid at the stylist's door were wheel spats (fender skirts), smaller wheels and their alarming side-effects on braking performance, deep alligator bonnets with tricky access (the Jaguar Mk.VII was a bad offender), and large areas of non-detachable sheet metal capable of turning apparently superficial damage into an insurance write-off. Those who derided the 2CV Citroën's "garden shed" look should remember that, by contrast, almost everything save the basic skeleton was demountable for quick and cheap replacement. Not that the stylist

(*Below*) A tradition fades. Britain's first razor-edge sedans were seen in 1935–36, and the idiom persisted through the 1950s, with Austin and Triumph applying it to volume-production cars. By contrast, the Empress body created by Royal coachbuilder Hooper for the 2.5-litre Special Sports Daimler chassis was a true special-order item, and a clever blend of the traditional shape with the latest in fender lines. A single-panel curved screen is used, though the headlamps are only half-recessed and even a minor parking incident would lead to alarming repair bills. This example from 1953 is mounted on the later 3.5-litre Regency chassis, a bigger six retaining Daimler's fluid flywheel preselective transmission as used by the company since 1930. Only about thirty such cars were built.

(*Opposite, top*) When this Tipo 410 Superfast coupé was exhibited at the 1956 Paris Salon, Ferraris were still being built on a truly bespoke basis. Created by Pininfarina (who else?), it was strictly a one-off, but total production of the 410 series did not exceed two dozen units, all with 5-litre V-12 engines delivering 340 horsepower at 6,000 rpm. There was still only one overhead camshaft per bank of cylinders and four forward speeds, while Enzo Ferrari—like most specialist makers—was content with a beam-axle rear end and drum brakes. Price? The 67,000 francs quoted in Switzerland for a "standard" 410 would have all but bought two Aston Martins, or three XK Jaguars with all the optional extras.

(*Opposite, bottom*) Not quite the ultimate in conventionally engineered "street" Ferraris—the Daytona was yet to come—but the best you could buy in 1966, a 275 GTB/4 *berlinetta* on the short, 2.4-m (7.9-ft) wheelbase. Split-circuit power disc brakes are becoming the norm for super-cars, but now Ferrari have switched to independent rear springing and a five-speed transaxle incorporating a limited-slip differential. The V-12 engine has the familiar dimensions of 77×58.8 mm (3,286 cc), but now there are twin overhead camshafts per bank of cylinders, six Weber dual-choke carburettors, and 300 horsepower, to give the happy customer 155 mph (250 km/h) and an acceleration over a quarter mile (0.4 km) in 14.7 seconds from standstill. Despite a production run of only two years, 280 such cars found buyers.

always had things his own way. An integrated body design could be changed only after it had paid for its tooling, and the weaker brethren suffered accordingly. Kaiser's "1951" shape (actually on sale early in 1950) would probably have seen the firm beyond their collapse in 1955, but there was nothing Singer could do with the SM1500 of 1948, outmoded by 1952 and still with four more laboured years ahead of it. For the devotees of unitary construction, the going was even harder: no wonder Nash scrapped Hudson's six-year-old Stepdown when they took over in 1954.

To show the problems of a unitary shape, let us consider that hardy perennial, the Hillman Minx, from a company that kept free of financial stress for at least the first eleven years of our period, with an annual sales potential of 50,000 or more at all times. Having gone unitary ahead of the rest in 1940, it lasted for the whole of our relevant twenty years. Yet, during this interval, it had precisely five shapes, one being the supplementary "Super" line produced alongside the basic Minx from 1962 to 1966. The final pre-war idiom took it through to 1948, when the slab-sided "squashed Plymouth" type took over. By dint of extensive juggling with chromium strip, enlarged boots, new grilles, and two-toning, this type held up until the summer of 1956. Detroit's latest "sculptured line" then enjoyed a ten-year heyday, while tail fins

came and went. The design was stretched into 1966 by giving it a razor-edge roofline (not unattractive), and a similar treatment was accorded to the bigger Supers for their last two seasons. The final wedge shape, common to both junior and senior models, emerged in 1966 and had a run of over ten years. Indeed, it was still being made in 1982 from British-built units in a state-owned factory in Iran.

Even such ingenious methods called for some sacrifices. There were no convertibles after 1964, and the operation was kept profitable by the intrusion of the badge-engineering element. Almost everything made after 1955 had close relatives which were either Sunbeams, Humbers, or Singers. Confusion might arise: the Super Minx-based Humber Sceptre of 1963 looked as if it had started as a Sunbeam only to be diverted into the prestige family by the addition of quad headlights (a Humber hallmark) and overdrive as standard. But to Britons, the Hillman Minx was an institution—it was not to anyone else, despite a healthy export performance from 1948 until the early sixties. Alas, it was too British in concept to challenge true world cars like the VW, the 403 and 404 Peugeots, or even the Mini. Further, the Minx had no stylistic continuity. Even had the final version less painfully resembled the latest in European Fords, it was by no means clearly a descendant of the 1950 car, let alone of its 1940 ancestor.

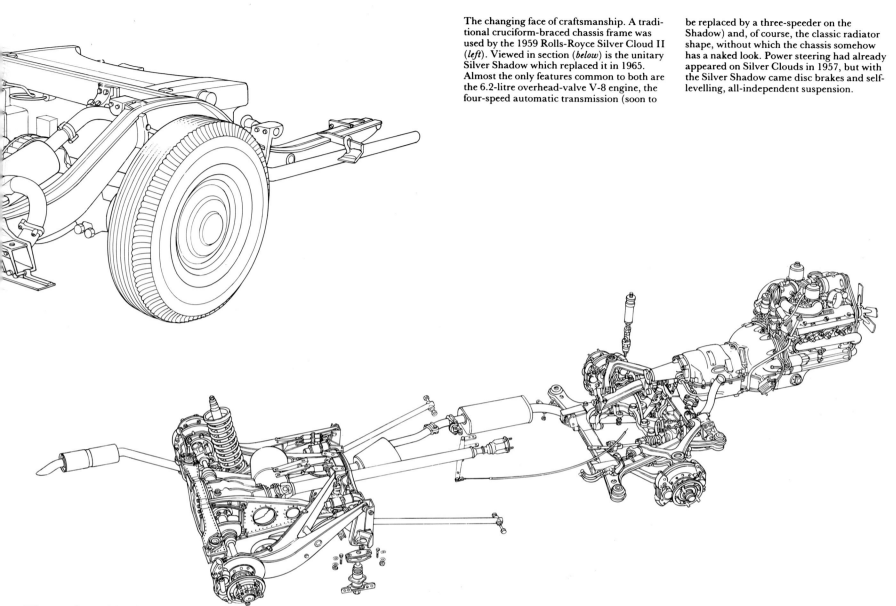

The changing face of craftsmanship. A traditional cruciform-braced chassis frame was used by the 1959 Rolls-Royce Silver Cloud II (*left*). Viewed in section (*below*) is the unitary Silver Shadow which replaced it in 1965. Almost the only features common to both are the 6.2-litre overhead-valve V-8 engine, the four-speed automatic transmission (soon to be replaced by a three-speeder on the Shadow) and, of course, the classic radiator shape, without which the chassis somehow has a naked look. Power steering had already appeared on Silver Clouds in 1957, but with the Silver Shadow came disc brakes and self-levelling, all-independent suspension.

Those who achieved an immortal shape—such as the Morris Minors of 1949–71, or the Volkswagen (born 1938 and still going strong in 1982, though not in Germany)—had to go into a great deal of detail work in keeping it up-to-date. Surviving specimens of Adolf Hitler's original KdF-Wagen in museums are unmistakable cousins of the latest models from Mexico or Brazil, but no part is interchangeable. A closer look reveals that the only common elements are the general shape, the "phut-phut" exhaust note, and the base engineering except for post-1969 suspensions. Even if we take the Beetle as it was in 1950, ignoring purely technical developments like synchromesh and disc front brakes, we begin with a small-windowed sedan, innocent of ventipanes or scuttle-vents. The thin bumpers sprouted overriders of dubious utility, the windscreen was straight rather than curved, and the rear window was of divided type, while the car rode on 16-in wheels. Scuttle air-vents came in 1951, front-window ventipanes in 1952, and an oval one-piece rear window in 1953. The latter gave way from 1957 to something bigger, no longer oval, and the window area was substantially increased in 1964. Anything made from 1954 onward had twin exhaust tailpipes, sliding roofs replaced the original canvas-insert option in 1962, and the "spine" on the rear engine cover disappeared in 1963. This is only a very abridged account of the changes.

The Morris Minor story is simpler: the shape was even more inflexible, and world demand had fallen off by the later 1950s. Changes made after 1949 included raised, semi-exposed headlamps (to conform with American law) in 1950, a new grille in 1953, and a single-panel curved screen from late 1956. The engine alterations of 1952, 1956, and 1962 had, in themselves, no significant effect on the Minor's appearance. Other long-lived shapes existed, too, in a period of stylistic change. The Alfa Romeo coupé and spyder of 1954–55, Fiat's 600 and 1100–103, the compact Jaguar sedans, the original Saab: all were at least fifteen years old by 1969, although both Fiats and the Jaguar were near the end of their careers. Oddly for such a period, it is a list as impressive as that of pre-war ancients still with us in 1955—the Citroën *traction* (1934), the IFA F8 *née* DKW Meisterklasse (1935), and that quartet from 1936, the Fiat 500, Type 170 Mercedes-Benz, T-type MG, and four-wheeled Morgan.

As we moved into the middle sixties, the stylist's function changed. In the early years, it was a case either of prolonging an outmoded shape's career, or ensuring that next year's model didn't look too like last year's. Pontiac's famed Silver Streaks, still around in 1956, had come into being twenty-two years earlier as a hurried add-on, for just this reason. But as the safety lobby moved in, the stylist's aid was

Sorrows of a stylist, or what can happen on a low budget. John Reinhart's new shape for the 1951 Packard was fine at its introduction, and still acceptable in 1952 (*left, top*): unfortunately it had to suffice, in essence, until 1956 and the end of the firm's independent technical existence. This one is, of course, a side-valve straight-eight, and the presence of only three ventilating ports in the rear fenders identifies it as the relatively inexpensive 4.7-litre 200 rather than the up-market 400. On this car, a three-speed manual transmission was standard, though over 85 % of Packards (less than 63,000 this year) preferred the company's own painless Ultramatic, and most of them would have chosen the servo-brake option, too. Still visible are traces of the traditional Packard radiator shape, crowned by the proud Cormorant mascot. Star of the 1954 range was the Caribbean convertible (*left, bottom*), still a straight-eight, though they'd extracted a startling 212 horsepower from 5.8 litres of engine, and there were nine main bearings as on the first of the family way back in 1923. The sporty Continental spare wheel kit was not the only built-in luxury—you also had power brakes, steering, top, seats, windows, and radio antenna, as well as automatic, a screenwash, and genuine wire wheels. At over $5,000 delivered, this monster attracted precisely 400 buyers.

(*Opposite, top*) Measures of desperation. Stuck with the ageing and whale-like Stepdown shape on their full-size cars, Hudson tried their luck with the compact Jet in 1953, on a 105-in (2.7-m) wheelbase. At long last, the traditional wet-plate clutch gave way to a dry-plate unit, but the engine, though now pressure-lubricated, was a modest 3.3-litre side-valve six giving only 114 horsepower even with a twin-carburettor ("Miracle H-Power"!) option. Sales of 35,000-odd in two seasons were not encouraging and, when Hudson merged with Nash to form American Motors, the new combine discarded the Jet in favour of Nash's established Rambler.

(*Opposite, bottom*) Unkind critics likened its styling to a "squashed Ford Consul", its unitary hull was corrosion-prone, and the transmission-type handbrake was an anachronism. But the 1100–103 Fiat unveiled in 1953 was one of the best small sedans of its era, good for over 75 mph (120 km/h), cruising at 70 mph (112 km/h) on its native *autostrade*, and turning in a frugal 38 mpg (7.4 litres/100 km). It was also fun to drive, and more flexible than the original *millecento*, on which skilled bootcraft had been necessary to sustain anything as low as 20 mph (31 km/h) in top. The central spotlamp identifies this as a second-series car from 1956–57.

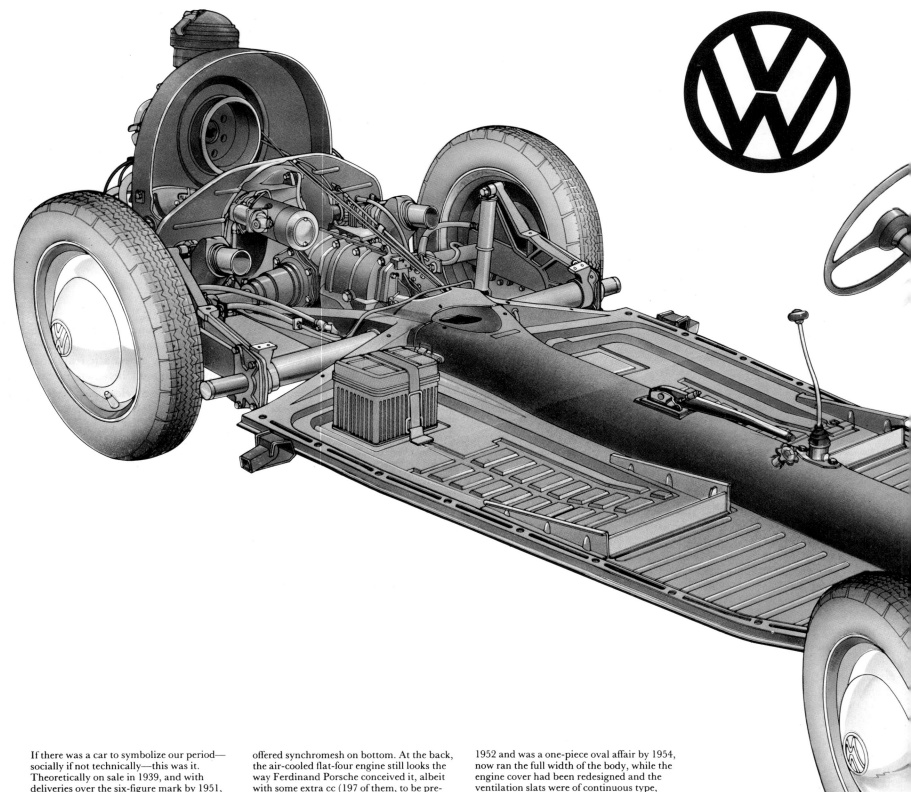

If there was a car to symbolize our period—socially if not technically—this was it. Theoretically on sale in 1939, and with deliveries over the six-figure mark by 1951, the Volkswagen *Käfer* would achieve its first million in August, 1955, and its tenth million just over ten years later, by which time rear engines were out of fashion and air-cooling was less popular as well. Exactly when it broke the Model-T Ford's production record is still a matter for debate, but by late 1981 world-wide deliveries exceeded twenty million units. Here (*above*) is a 1958-model chassis as today's kit-car fraternity sees it: a tubular backbone frame with torsion-bar springing at either end, rack-and-pinion steering, and the familiar cranked central gear lever controlling four forward speeds, although it will be another two years before buyers are

offered synchromesh on bottom. At the back, the air-cooled flat-four engine still looks the way Ferdinand Porsche conceived it, albeit with some extra cc (197 of them, to be precise, since 1939) and 30 horsepower instead of 23, which spell maximum *and* cruising speeds of 112 km/h (70 mph). Brakes are hydraulic, too, though until 1962 the parsimonious could order a "stripped" model with mechanically actuated cables! The sectioned side view of a complete car (*opposite, top*) is a trifle claustrophobic by 1980s standards, and the maker's ideas of luggage accommodation also seem a little optimistic. They did stress the value of proper weight distribution with a low centre of gravity, and the better traction obtained by placing the engine directly over the drive wheels. The rear window, which had still been divided in

1952 and was a one-piece oval affair by 1954, now ran the full width of the body, while the engine cover had been redesigned and the ventilation slats were of continuous type, illustrating the host of minor changes which marked the Beetle's steady evolution. The 1954 power pack (*opposite, centre*) shows the big shrouded cooling-fan mounted in front of the engine, with its driving-belt at the rear. The carburettor is very accessible: the lower spark-plugs less so. Ten years later, the rear window was even larger, you could open the engine cover by pressing a button rather than turning a handle, and the tail-light cluster had been revised too. There wasn't a lot of space under the frontal "bonnet" (*opposite, bottom*), either, after allowing for the spare wheel and the fuel tank—but accessory roof-racks were quite cheap.

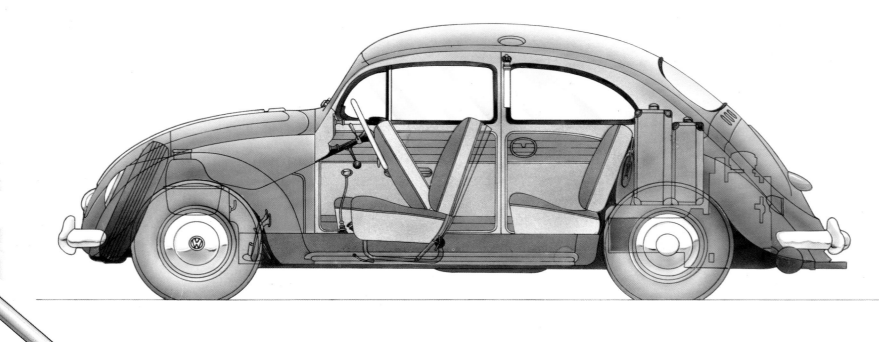

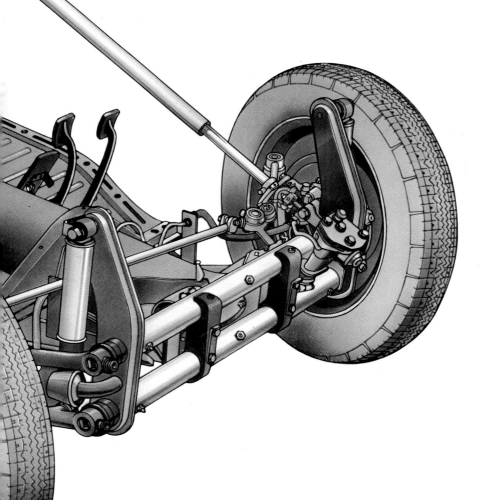

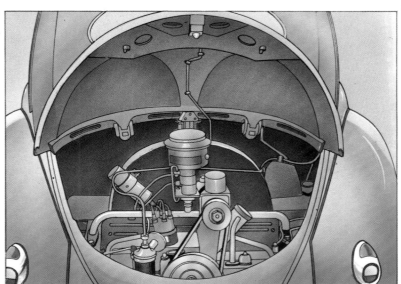

path. His motives were technical and sentimental rather than stylistic. If one had to market three family sedans under three different names in the same group, it was cheaper to play with grilles, interior trim, and two-toning than with engines, suspensions, and body shells. The British Motor Corporation, the worst offenders of this kind, entered 1955 with four distinct 1,500-cc family sedans. Admittedly, they used the same engines and transmissions, but they ran to three totally different chassis/body structures, while front suspensions were divided between the Austin type (coils) and Morris's torsion bars. Sometimes, badge engineering was of the crudest sort: the sole difference between the original 1959 Austin Se7en (*sic*) and the Morris Mini-Minor (again *sic*) was the grille-bar pattern (straight on a Morris, wavy on an Austin), though the colour charts were not the same.

Carried to its logical conclusion—and one that was inevitable, given two dealership chains and two sets of entrenched *marque*-loyalty (in Britain, at any rate)—we reach the strange state of affairs which obtained from 1965 onward in the front-wheel-drive 1100/1300 line-up. Here we find five different grilles, three stages of engine tune, three levels of interior appointments with some further internal variations, and the ultimate nuisance of body permutations. The inflexibilities of unitary construction limited the choice to two- and four-door sedans and to station wagons, but all styles were not available on all brands of 1100 or 1300 and, at times, a variation permitted for export never appeared on the home market. A certain degree of "difference" was achieved, yet it must have been a nightmare for the stylists, and a worse one for production engineers who had to feed all the permutations down the assembly line. In the long run, one wonders if it was all really necessary.

The disease would naturally spread into Europe during the 1970s, with cross-pollinations of Audi/VW and Peugeot/Citroën among others. But it was never as uncontrolled as in Britain, and sometimes it even made sense. A joint development programme shared by Peugeot, Renault, and Volvo would breed an excellent V-6 engine which, in all probability, none of the individual contributors would have considered viable without outside backing. It is fair, however, to add that this went into three completely different cars.

As in America, so in Europe. Bumpers, grilles, lamps, running-boards, boots were gathered up and merged into harmonious wholes. The traditional running-board had all but gone by 1953 and, henceforward, the only excrescences to mar the shape of the motor car were wing mirrors and radio antennae, while even the last could be wound electrically out of sight by the mid-sixties. Fuel fillers were set flush in the rear quarters. The windscreen wipers, on 1967 American cars, were not only self-parking but vanished into a slot at the lower edge. Retractable headlamps, last seen on 1942's De Sotos, were back again in 1963 on the British Lotus Elan sports car, appearing on a variety of Americans—led by Buick—from 1965 onwards.

European sedan shapes generally followed the basic American idiom. Typical variations on the GM/Ford theme came in the early 1950s from Alfa Romeo, Austin, Fiat, British and German Fords, Mercedes-Benz, Opel, the Rootes Group, Rover, and Vauxhall. But Mercedes and, to a lesser extent, Alfa Romeo retained their traditional radiator grilles. Full wrap-round rear windows were not so popular, and largely confined to such American-controlled companies as Ford, Opel, and Vauxhall. These were, however, applied to a number of coupés, a fine example being the three-cylinder DKW of 1954 which, in its final form, boasted a dog's-leg windscreen as well.

European contributions to the quad-headlamp craze included an

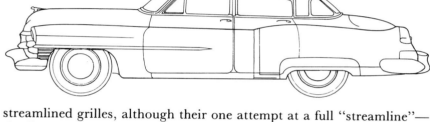

attractive variation, the vertical cluster used on Facel Vegas from 1954.
Among imitators of the American configuration were Humber, Ford of
Britain, Jaguar, and Lancia—plus, surprisingly, the Prince from Japan—in 1961, and Alfa Romeo in 1962. By 1963, even the aristocratic
Rolls-Royce and Alvis had succumbed to the fad, which was still
strongly supported in 1969. Fins, however, did not really fit in, and
none of the more outrageous interpretations from Detroit crossed the
Atlantic. Rootes, predictably, produced a watered-down variation on
the theme, as did Simca on their later V-8 Vedettes. Some rather
depressing appendages were found on such 1959 sports models as the
Auto Union 1000 Sp (a species of mini-Thunderbird in the original
1955 spirit) and Daimler's SP250, but they had no imitators.

Alongside the American echoes, old shapes lingered on for a few
years, especially in Britain. In 1951, the standard models from Alvis,
Citroën, Daimler, Lea-Francis, MG, Morgan, Riley, Rolls-Royce/Bent-
ley, and Singer (on roadsters only) retained both a traditional shape
and an unmistakable radiator grille. The same, to a lesser degree, went
for Lancia's sedans. Right up to 1955, Mercedes-Benz continued to
make the good old 170, complete with running-boards, exposed lamps,
and bumpers which looked like afterthoughts. The clean-up, however,
was on the way. Already Alvis ran to rear wheel spats and semi-reces-
sed headlamps, while the last of the traditional Jaguars, Mk.V, was
phased out during the summer of 1951 in favour of the slab-sided,
integrated Mk.VII. By 1952, integrated headlamps characterized the
latest Daimlers and Lanchesters, the Lea-Francis' headlamps having
already retreated into the wings. Catalogues for 1954 featured slab-
sided sedans from Mercedes-Benz, MG, and Riley. MG's new 1956
sports car, the MG-A, dispensed with running-boards, individual
wings, and a traditional radiator. Even Morgans acquired mildly

streamlined grilles, although their one attempt at a full "streamline"—
the Plus Four Plus coupé of 1963—met with such resistance from customers that it was withdrawn after a very short run. The classical
tractions outlived Citroën's Déesse by only twenty months, being
dropped in the summer of 1957.

Even some of the surviving "traditionals" were not as traditional as
they looked. Apart from its recessed headlamps, the 1951 Type 220 six-
cylinder Mercedes-Benz might have stepped straight out of the 1938
Berlin Show, but the conventional bonnet was afflicted with fixed sides
and an alligator top. In any case, the side-opening bonnet was ill-suited
to the new high wing lines, thus leaving motorists stuck with the tiresome alligator and its linkages: either via a wire protruding through the
grille, by pressure on the radiator badge, or by a remote-control knob
under the dash, this last being perhaps the commonest in later days, if
only because it was thief-proof. Better accessibility was sought on Aston
Martins and the post-1958 Triumphs (Herald, Vitesse, Spitfire) by
making the whole bonnet-wing assembly tilt forward, at the same time
exposing the front suspension. Alas, it let in road dirt, was prone to
distortion, and scarcely guarded against the ministrations of careless
filling-station attendants. The idea was not new—it had been used on
air-cooled Tatras as long ago as 1924.

But whatever the shape, there remained the question of amortization.
How many cars can one unload, how long will it take to unload them,
and will the whole concept be out of date before the appointed target
has been reached? By 1930s standards, tooling costs were horrific.
True, in 1932 Chrysler expended $9,000,000 (say £1,500,000) on
rebuilding the Plymouth plant, but this was a prelude to the switch
from four cylinders to six, and they would still be using essentially the
same engine twenty-six years later. At a simpler level, Daimler, unable

Three shapes of the 1950s. The original 1950 Saab 92 (*opposite, top*) is still a triumph of perfect aerodynamics over most other considerations, to be expected from one of Europe's leading aircraft manufacturers. Its engineering is improved DKW: 764-cc water-cooled twin two-stroke engine driving the front wheels, three-speed synchromesh transmission with free wheel, rack-and-pinion steering, and hydraulic brakes. Debits are poor headroom, negligible rearward vision, and fender skirts which are built-in mud traps, while customers could have it in any colour so long as it was this green. The shape, if not the engine, had nearly another thirty years to go, whereas Fiat's 500C (*below*) would be dropped in 1955 after a career dating back to 1936. With its hydraulic brakes, adequate legroom, four-speed synchromesh transmission, and independently sprung front wheels, the Fiat had been the baby-car to beat before World War II, and even in 1950—as seen here—it was still competitive, thanks to a redesigned 16.5-horsepower version of the old 570-cc engine with overhead valves. It could outrun the original side-valve Morris Minors of 1949–52, yet it was strictly a two-seater and something of a home mechanic's nightmare—everything looked so accessible, but fingers were not small enough! The "other Swede", Volvo (*opposite, bottom*), would go on making fastback variations on the PV444 theme (a 1944 debutante) into the mid-sixties. By 1957, this car was showing its age, too, with 1942 American styling (more Ford than anything else) and a three-speed transmission controlled by a long, willowy lever in the 1935 idiom. What it had, however, was a new performance image: capacity had been increased from the original 1,414 cc to 1,583 cc and, with an extra carburettor, there were 85 horsepower and 90 mph (145 km/h). The proof of the pudding was in the eating—this was the model that would spearhead the Gothenburg factory's successful onslaught on the tricky U.S. market.

Badge engineering, or pandering to out-moded marque loyalties. Throughout the 1960s, Britons—and some export customers—could buy this dull and dependable piece of Pininfarina styling with 1.5-litre engine, or 1.6-litre from 1961. The options listed included automatic, though never disc brakes, and in a few export markets the basic Austin/Morris version was available with a diesel engine. Here (*right*) we see the Austin Cambridge so beloved of family man and rural hire-car operator. The Morris Oxford was exactly the same thing with a different badge. But add a traditional grille, an illuminated radiator emblem, and some wood and leather within, and you have a Wolseley (*below*). More grille swapping and an extra carburettor give you a Riley or MG. The Australians lengthened the BMC-Farina theme and fitted their own brand of short-block six to produce local Austins and Wolseleys—and the strangest things happened in Argentina, including a "Riley Rural" pickup!

(*Opposite*) What concealed headlamps can do. Both cars are 1968 Chevrolet Camaros, General Motors' belated answer to the best-selling Ford Mustang coupés and convertibles. The SS (*left*) has a conventional installation, while the Rallye Sport (*right*) tucks its

illuminations away electrically into the grille when they are not in use. For all the names, the Rallye Sport was a "personality package" (mouldings round the wheel arches, special emblem on the fuel-filler cap) rather than a sporting one: you had to specify one of the hairier V-8s if you wanted speed and acceleration. The SS, by contrast, came as stock with a 5.7-litre or 6.5-litre V-8, the latter rated at 325 horsepower. With this engine, you also had your rear body panel painted black, presumably to alert the Highway Patrol!

to subsist on chauffeur-driven limousines in the Depression years, spent a mere £30,000 ($180,000) on tooling up for their small 1.2-litre Lanchester in 1932, giving themselves a natural seller in the retired-colonel market.

Daimler's economics were entirely healthy. They could reasonably hope to sell 3,000–4,000 a year, and the clientele was conservative. It appreciated the preselective gearbox—for which, in any case, Daimler were tooled—but was disinterested in sophisticated suspensions or in the impending "streamline" craze. History records that the first cars had hydraulic brakes, scrapped quite soon in favour of cheaper mechanicals, but it is unlikely that the customers noticed. With a fairly wide range of body styles on a straightforward chassis, Daimler made it through to World War II with a single major restyle in 1937, although a full updating was planned for 1941 and was duly released as a post-war model in 1945. This sufficed till 1951, but the next step would have to be unitary construction—with some improvements in transmission, meaning an automatic. Worse still, the planned size of 1.6 litres implied that there could be very little interchangeability of parts with the next larger model, a 2.5-litre six. Thus, on top of an untried mechanical recipe, they were saddled with a complete retooling programme, which would have cost £500,000 ($1,400,000) with no guarantee of selling enough cars before the shape became outmoded. The limit seemed to be 8,000 a year in the overcrowded and capricious English upper-middle-class market, and this car was hardly something for the export customer. So the Lanchester Sprite went to the wall after about ten prototypes had been built. The cost per copy is best left to the imagination.

As an indication of what a mass producer could spend, Plymouth's next big factory update in 1955 cost $40,000,000, and a reorganization of the Buick plant took $500,000,000 in pursuit of a million-a-year production schedule as yet unrealized in 1982. Even facelifts called for deep pockets. It cost Jaguar £250,000 to bring the E-type into line with the American safety and emission standards enforced in 1968. Hence, spending the money on the wrong car could be catastrophic: classic instances of this were Kaiser's Henry J compact (1950), Borgward's 1959 big six (confronting Mercedes-Benz), and the Hillman Imp (1963).

People still wanted a choice of bodies. Convertibles were a constant source of worry, as a maker had no room for side-issues even where he was responsible for his own pressings. Ford used Carbodies in Britain and went to Karosserie Deutsch in Germany, while VW drew on Karmann, Opel on Autenrieth, BMW and Auto Union on Baur. The British Jensen company, originally coachbuilders, revived their old love to supplement a meagre production of cars, building ragtops for BMC (Austin, Austin-Healey), the open Alpines of 1959–68 for Rootes, and Volvo's P1800 coupés until 1963 for the Gothenburg firm.

The convertible would become a major casualty of the decade. Even a separate chassis required some reinforcement to circumvent scuttle-shake, and unitaries were far trickier—as Citroën had discovered to their cost in 1934, when they offered a roadster in the original *traction* range. One way out, long favoured in Germany on both separate-chassis and unitary models, was the cabrio-limousine, on which the body sides were fixed, leaving only a roll-top roof. In our period, such a style was marketed by Fiat, Nash, Opel, Peugeot, and Renault, while examples with chassis included the original Fiat 500. It was an acceptable compromise, but the lines were still the sedan's. Further, the demand for convertibles was limited: in 1955, the all-car/ragtop totals produced by Chevrolet, Ford, and Plymouth were respectively 1,830,029/66,121, 1,451,157/41,966, and 742,991/8,473. The market was being eroded from various directions. In America, the two-door hardtop coupé, with all the style and none of the snags, sold better—for all the "wind in your hair" nonsense purveyed by advertising agencies, the ladies did not care to subject their hairdos to freeway speeds. Even the soft-topped sports car was disappearing. Where Lancia had begun, others carried on the good work. Jaguar and Porsche, who offered both styles of body, always did better overall with closed models. The conclusion was obvious before the safety-propagandists stepped in.

Open sports cars, of course, saw the second decade out. The Triumph Spitfire and TR6, the E-type Jaguar roadster, and the MG-B were still going strong in 1969, as were Italy's open Alfa Romeos and Fiats. The defection of Datsun and Porsche, however, did not pass unnoticed, while the non-sporting convertible was fading out. Such cars as the Singer Roadster (1951–55) and the Austin A40 Sports (1951–53)

(*Below*) Ford of America's new look—Phase One, the 1951 Mercury Club Coupé, complete with coil-spring independent front suspension (new, incredibly, as late as 1949) and hypoid rear axle. The cruciform-braced frame on this car is of course Lincoln rather than Ford in origin, while already the divided windscreen and bulbous fender treatment are looking a trifle outmoded. And whereas GM and Chrysler have V-8s with upstairs valves and oversquare dimensions, Mercury's engine is still an antiquated side-valve offering 110 horsepower from 4.2 litres. Further, GM have now had automatics for eleven years, but this is the first season they will be available on either Ford or Mercury.

(*Opposite, top*) Amazing grace—or a stylistic elegance seldom achieved by Americans—on the second-year edition of Raymond Loewy's brilliant 1953 Studebaker Commander coupé. The 1954 is hard to distinguish from the earlier models, and chromium-plated ornamentation is kept to a minimum. The company's V-8 (3.8 litres, 120 horsepower) was modest if adequate, but triumph was turned into disaster by problems of corrosion, poor quality control, costly experiments with mechanical power steering (some assistance was needed, for the Commander required nearly six turns from lock to lock), and bad planning. Studebaker intended the coupé as a limited-production "come on" to attract customers into the showroom—and then sell sedans. When the demand arrived, there were not enough coupés to go round. And by 1955, the chromium plate was moving in ...

(*Opposite, bottom*) American Motors sought escape from their "common sense" image in the 1960s, this Marlin (originally badged as a Rambler in 1965) being an entry for the personal-car market. Looks of this 1966 version were individual enough, but it was a big car on a 112-in (2.85-m) wheelbase, and its length of 195 in (4.05 m) made it a handful beside Ford's Mustang. The standard engine was, predictably, a staid 3.8-litre pushrod six, but with the optional 5.4-litre V-8 the Marlin was a respectable performer. Its whale-like styling was, however, against it, and steadily diminishing sales told their own story. In three seasons, only 17,500 customers chose this one.

were not very saleable in their heyday and would have been dead ducks in the climate of, say, 1966.

In 1960, most relevant German and American manufacturers still had something in this class, as did Fiat in Italy, BMC, Ford, and Rootes in Britain, or Peugeot and Simca in France. But the market was dwindling, and a maker committed to unitary construction was likely to think twice about tooling for a convertible the next time a redesign became due. Few firms did so, and even in America the boom was almost over. If Chrysler's ragtop sales remained steady throughout the sixties at 4,000–5,000 a year, Buick—the top American builder of convertibles—saw orders slip from 41,528 in 1962 to 22,616 in 1969. Ford, admittedly, disposed of 33,874 cars in the latter year, but this was only just over half 1962's showing. Most indicative of the decline is the story of the Ford Mustang, a car which seemed a natural for the "sporty ragtop" clientele: 73,112 convertibles were sold in 1965, the model's first full year, but less than 15,000 found buyers in the last season of our period. European factories encountered the same picture. In the Triumph Herald/Vitesse family, the convertibles accounted for about 11 % of sales (with no ultimate competition in Britain), but Peugeot's 2 % ration of coupés in the 204 and 404 ranges included hardtops as well, and the same went for Mercedes-Benz's statistics at 6 % of all medium-sized sixes up to 1965.

Colour was assuming greater and greater importance. It was used to inject an extra year of life into the ageing 1949 Hillman Minx shape, and now the dual aids of colour and chromium were pressed into service: plated strip, sweep-spears and, later, sculptured lines could divide one shade from another. Sometimes the results were alarming, as on Ford of America's 1955 Crown Victoria, "with a crown of chrome

sweeping down from roof to belt line at center pillar level". On the 1956 De Soto Fireflite, something resembling an attenuated rifle (in contrasting colour) started low down by the rear bumper, taking in the rear wheel arch as a "trigger guard", the "barrel" terminating in a stylus-shaped "head" just behind the front wheels. This set off the new six-window styling and tail fins quite well, but was hardly beautiful. Chrysler's colour-influences spilled over into later Simca Arondes, although Citroën did it better on the Déesse by painting their glass-fibre roof section in a lighter shade. In Britain, two-tone treatment was skilfully applied to some of the uglier examples of slab-sided styling—Austin's A105, Ford's Mk.I Zodiac, and Standard's Pennant and Vanguard. Here the lily was sometimes gilded by minor engine tuning, in addition to a goodly quota of accessories. Ford's 1954 Zodiac package included white-wall tyres, heater, screenwash, wing mirrors, clock, and reversing lamps, as well as two-tone paint. The little Standard Pennant was embellished with a wider grille and headlamp hoods.

A lot could be done with wheels, almost invariably plain discs except where brake-cooling problems dictated otherwise. Perhaps the most fashionable accessory of the 1940s had been the "beauty ring" (Britons called it a "rimbellisher"), a painted or chromed rim trim, originally devised in the U.S.A. at a time when white-wall tyres were still hard to get. Wire wheels were too expensive, and chromium plating on the spokes was liable to weaken them, so America succumbed during the middle fifties to a fad for clip-on dummy wire trims. On the 1953 Buick Skylark, however, genuine wires with "40 individually set chromed spokes" were standard equipment, which explains why it cost $1,000 more than any other car in the range and sold in tiny numbers. Also imitated were the cast magnesium-alloy spoked wheels used on compe-

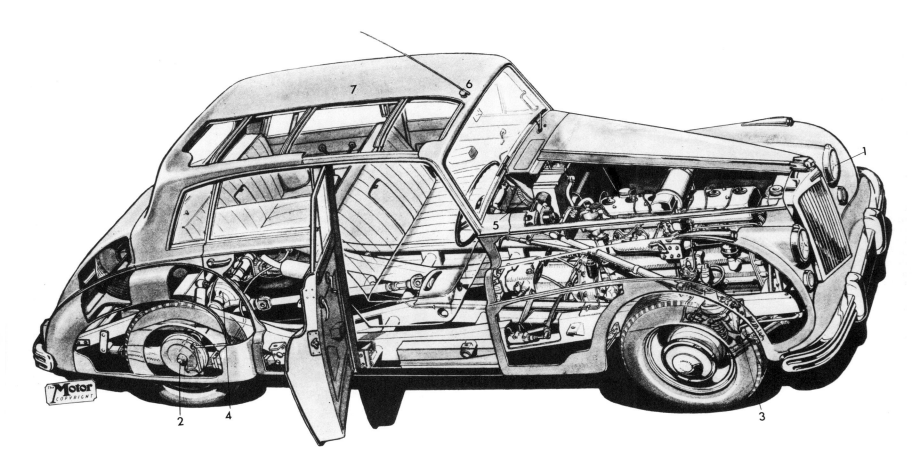

106

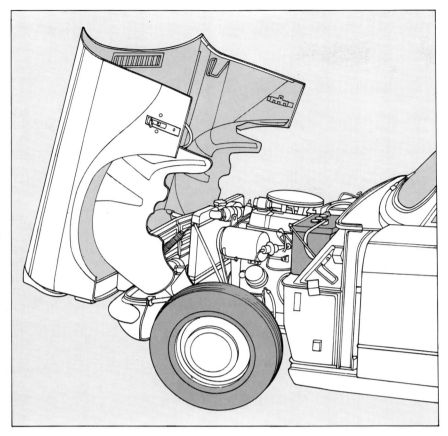

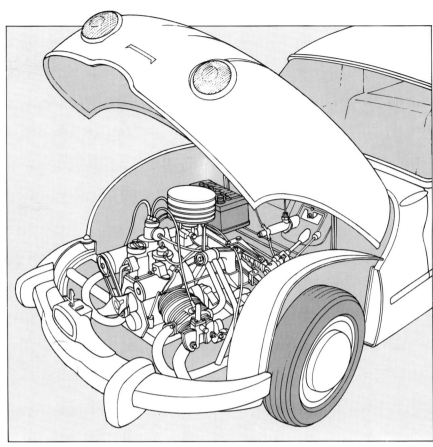

(*Opposite*) Eliminate (*1*) the recessed headlamps, (*2*) the hydraulic brakes, and (*3*) the coil-spring independent suspension, replacing the hypoid rear axle (*4*) with an old-fashioned spiral bevel, and we could be back in the Britain of 1938 with this 3.4-litre Armstrong Siddeley Sapphire as made from 1953 to 1958. True, the six-cylinder engine has hemispherical combustion chambers and the "square" dimensions of 90×90 mm, and by pre-war standards 120 horsepower would be a lot from a power unit of this capacity. Students of creature comforts will note the heater trunking (*5*) and radio antenna (*6*), while the roof (*7*) lacks that sliding panel found on almost all British sedans of the 1930s. But one did get two-speed wipers, a fuel reserve, a map-reading light, and wood and leather trim, while Armstrong Siddeley's preselective transmission (still available as an alternative to synchromesh) now had its ratios electrically selected. From 1955 there would be an automatic option, too. Rover, Jaguar, and Mercedes-Benz would, however, be the death of the smaller specialist makers, although Armstrong Siddeley also tried their luck in 1955 with a seven-seater limousine on which radio and an electric division were standard. Alas, there were not enough mayors and company presidents to keep the order-books full, while undertakers tended to buy secondhand.

(*Above*) Better under-hood access, but for road dirt as well as the home mechanic. On the 1959 Triumph Herald (*left*) the entire hood/fender assembly tilts forward, being secured by fasteners at its trailing edge. By contrast, that of the 1954 Dyna-Panhard sedan (*right*) hinges fom the back, in a fashion pioneered by Tatra of Czechoslovakia a good twenty years previously. This is a real boon on a front-wheel-drive car, and in any case the air-cooled Panhard has no "plumbing". Better still, the inner "wings" keep some of the dirt out. This remarkable little car featured all-aluminium unitary construction, which produced a full six-seater capable of 120 km/h (75 mph) and a frugal 7 litres/100 km (40 mpg) all on 850 cc and two cylinders. Heavy manufacturing costs, alas, caused a switch to steel bodies in 1957, and the extra weight didn't help the handling. The Panhard was always a noisy little car and, though *la marque doyenne*'s annual sales were up to over 30,000 in the late fifties, this wasn't enough for a small, cheap family model. A Citroën takeover in 1955 was only the prelude to the disappearance of the Panhard name twelve years later.

tition cars from the later fifties. A prevalent disease of the 1970s, these were very much with us from 1967–68 onward, finding their way onto MG Midgets among others. The "Ro style" label commemorated their initial use by Rover on the 1968 eight-cylinder line.

Britain's Ford Zodiac and its fellows sparked off another strong trend of the 1960s. If a body programme was inflexible and restricted one to sedans and station wagons, one could still offer quite a wide range of models by graduated trim packages, with or without mechanical modifications thrown in. When hanging a "GT" label on a car, something would have to be done to the engine, but a good deal of variety could be achieved by the French-type graduations of equipment. *Affaires* gave a minimal specification, and *Confort* was not always very much better. At the other end of the scale were GL (*Grand Luxe*) and GLS (*Grand Luxe Special*, or maybe *Sport*—one consulted the catalogue to discover which it was). On Simca's front-wheel-drive 1100 (1968), a GL model came complete with rear overriders, two vanity mirrors instead of one, armrests at front and rear, a parcel shelf, child-proof door locks, and a grab-handle: a judicious mixture of safety and luxury. In the GLS grouping, you got some ornament as well—mild scriptitis at both ends, plus reclining front seats, rim trims, through-flow ventilation, a thermometer, a clock, a second grab-handle, rear-seat ashtrays, coat hooks, a lockable glove-compartment, and floor carpets instead of rubber mats.

Vinyl roof-coverings were fashionable from about 1961, to make a sedan look like a hardtop. They were standard on Humber's 1965 Imperial to distinguish the car from the cheaper, but otherwise identical, Super Snipe. On the 1968 Dodge Charger, however, you could have your vinyl in "black, antique white, or antique green", this being but one of a whole series of dress-up kits offered. As the Dodge could be had with engines giving over 400 horsepower, sporty items predominated. Comprehensive (extra) instrumentation included a rev-counter "large

(*Left*) Secondhand American influences. On Vauxhall's Cresta PA, marketed from 1958 to 1960, we encounter a 2.3-litre six-cylinder overhead-valve engine and classic unitary construction of the type used by this company since 1938. But now the stylists have added a dog's-leg windscreen—though a neater one than on the companion four-cylinder Victor family—along with tail fins, and even the three-piece wrap-round rear window found elsewhere only on 1957 Buicks. The PA family ran through to 1962, but during a fairly brief life it used two different wheel sizes and three patterns of radiator grille, while in 1961 it was given bigger fins and a bigger engine. By this time, too, overdrive and automatic were available as well as the all-too-familiar three on the column.

(*Opposite, bottom*) The British Ford Consul II convertible as made from 1956 to 1962 (this is a '59) looks less spectacular in the metal than it did in the company's catalogues. The shorter hood, of course, does not help: the more expensive Zephyrs and Zodiacs had 2.6-litre in-line sixes instead of the Consul's 1.7-litre four. Ford managed a unitary convertible by having Carbodies of Coventry do a top chop. On the cheaper four-cylinder cars, this component went up and down by hand. As power assistance on the sixes took it only halfway, not a lot was lost, though in an affluent society the sixes now outsold the fours. In Mk. I days (1951–56), the ratio was 4-to-3 in favour of the Consul.

(*Opposite, top*) Last new Jaguar model with a separate chassis, the Mk. IX sedan (1958). There's not a lot to distinguish it externally from the original Mk.VII of 1950 save the single-panel windscreen, and nothing to show that it's not a 1957 Mk.VIII. But in eight years, power has gone up by 40 % to 220 horsepower, top speed up by 10 % to 113 mph (179 km/h), and 0–60 mph (0–100 km/h) acceleration figures have improved by 20 %. Add power disc brakes on all four wheels (no mixed systems for Jaguar!) and power steering, and you have a luxury carriage that will still keep pace with the American opposition even if it lacks tail fins. Automatic, compulsory for the U.S. market, is only one of three options (the others are manual and manual/overdrive) elsewhere. Sales of 10,000 Mk.IXs in three seasons were entirely satisfactory: after all, the makers had their profitable compact sedans, and the XK150 sports car destined to give way during 1961 to the advanced E-type.

(*Right*) A touch of Pininfarina made all the difference to Austin's small conventional sedan announced at the 1958 Shows, a year ahead of the Mini. The A40's mechanics are copybook British: 948-cc (or 1,098-cc from 1961) pushrod four-cylinder engine, four-speed synchromesh transmission, unitary construction, coil springs at the front and semi-elliptics at the rear. The wider track not only improved the looks—it eliminated the old A35's penchant for lying down on its door handles! The two-tone finish helped to make up for what the little Austin lacked in character, and so did a modest 42-mpg (7 litres/100 km) thirst for fuel. This was the first British Motor Corporation design to be made under licence in Italy by Innocenti.

enough so you can read it", as did "mag-style covers" (our old friend the Ro-style wheel again) and "bold, brash bumblebee stripes on the tail". A steering-wheel in "simulated woodgrain" was an attraction at a time when wood-rim wheels were regularly worn on Maseratis and the like.

The package business reached its zenith on the sportier Fords of the 1960s, the American Mustang and the Anglo-German Capri (1969). "Packs" were not to be classed with accessories, which had to be ordered individually and were supplementary to a wide choice of engine/transmission combinations (six in Germany). There were cosmetic and performance "packs". With the XL order came reclining front seats, separately contoured rear seats, an extra rear lamp, and an anti-dazzle mirror. XLRs were XLs with leather-rimmed steering-wheels, simulated black leather gearshift knobs, and map-reading lights. It must have been some compensation to a client who could not help being aware that his Capri was one of a million look-alikes with the same chassis/body, the same wheelbase, and essentially the same instrumentation.

Italy had her dress-up industry, too, although this was secondary to the nation's vast influence on overall styling from the early fifties onward. Up to 1950, America had been the style leader in the mass-produced sector. Formal car ranges might be inspired by the British razor-edge idiom of 1935 on; the beautifully made, if somewhat ponderous, German cabriolet style had its echoes in Sweden and Switzerland; and the splendid, if impractical, sporting roadster with flowing wings and a windscreen of letterbox-slot proportions hailed from France. But when it came to cheap sedans, be they Renaults, Opels, or Austins, they still reflected secondhand U.S. thinking, usually distorted by its adaptation to shorter wheelbases and abbreviated bonnets. Italy's main influence so far had been confined to open sporting bodywork: Zagato's magnificent Gran Sport Alfa Romeo of 1929 remained the exemplar of this type of coachwork up to 1936–37.

The new "tin" of the forties and early fifties was still strongly Detroit-oriented. Singer aped Kaiser, and so did Volvo on a V-8 prototype which never saw production. Standard and Rootes drew their inspiration from two successive generations of Plymouth, the original Austin A40 was a stunted 1940 Chevrolet, and the Borgward 1500 was a deplorable mixture of American and German thinking. Renault's Frégate and Fiat's 1400 had no obvious American prototypes, yet were clearly non-European in concept. Ironically, Hudson would borrow back from Fiat for their unsuccessful compact Jet sedan of 1953. Volvo mixed GM grilles, Ford front wings, and Chrysler's body shapes to produce some astonishing mock-Americans: a definite style would not emerge until the 140 series (1966). Even the successful and well-loved 120 series (1956 onward) had front ends which were pure 1955 Chrysler. The Japanese, handicapped by a sheet-steel shortage, continued to build bodies by hand, the end product having assorted Chrysler, GM, and Crosley overtones. The 1951 Datsun, indeed, could have been confused with one of Powel Crosley's diminutive overhead-camshaft sedans.

This state of affairs made up in variety for what it lacked in elegance or cohesion. That is, until the Italians moved in, adopting the British razor-edge idiom and refining it beyond the narrow confines of Anglo-Saxon imagination. Given separate wings and headlamps, and a proper radiator, Britons could achieve low-cost miracles, such as the big Triumph sedans of the 1946–54 era. But let the concept of integration take over, and one encounters disasters like the 1.3-litre Triumph Mayflower, summarized by an unkind woman journalist as having "a Queen Anne top and a Mary Anne bottom".

Led by Pininfarina, the Italians championed the retreat from the shibboleths of the chassis maker's front-end treatment. Some of the

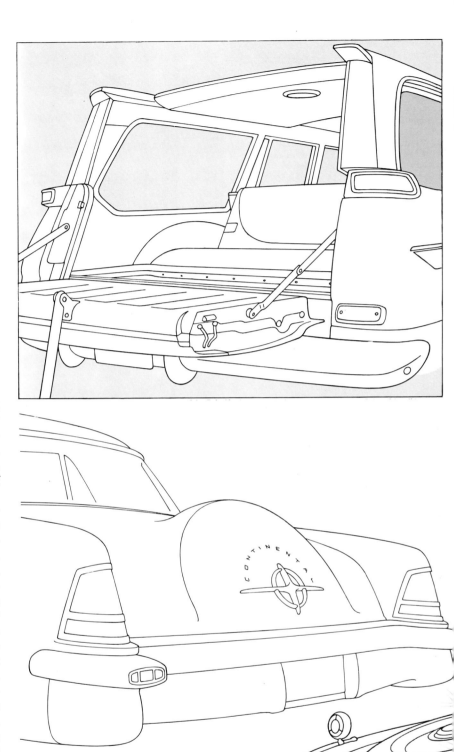

(*Top*) Refining the wagon. The 1963 Studebaker Lark Wagonaire had a one-piece tailgate as standard: options included a folding ladder for access to the roof, a power-operated rear window, and the sun-roof (helpful for indivisible loads, too). A luggage rack for the roof, and a folding extra seat in the rear, could also be obtained. Even the floor of the cargo area was carpeted, and washable vinyl interior surfaces helped.

Nostalgia before the nostalgia-car, or the cult of the Continental spare wheel kit, looked right on the original Mk.I Continental Lincoln, styled by E.T. Gregorie for Edsel Ford, and current in the 1940–48 period. Typical of the revival was Nash's version (*above*), widely applied to their cars in the 1950s and here seen on the British-made 1.2-litre Metropolitan coupé of 1954. But when Lincoln went nostalgic and revived the Continental theme as Mk. II for 1956, (*opposite, centre*), it was merely a trunk lid pressing, and looked it.

Chrysler (*below*) approached the theme from a sportier angle, with a realistic and not unattractive pressing on the K310 "dream car" created for them by Ghia of Italy in 1952. This one came close to actual production, though one wonders if the Corporation could have afforded the wire wheels—genuine, not clip-on trims. The only concrete result was, of course, 1957's infamous "dust-bin lid", or "sportdeck", as Chrysler preferred to call it.

early outbursts of rebellion were fairly horrible, since they drew on such unsuccessful purveyors of grille-work as Buick, Lincoln, and Studebaker. Nonetheless, the vee-grilles used—with a marked lack of discrimination—by Ghia and Pininfarina on Alfa Romeos, Lancias, and Fiats in 1937–39 were standardized on 1940's bigger Fiat models, and would survive on the old-school 508C Millecento until early 1953. But while the seller's market remained, the Italians had little chance to work on foreign chassis. They could neither import these, nor export bodies to European clients, except for subsequent re-export to hard-currency countries. Before 1951, the sole signs of outside work had been bodies by Touring and Pininfarina on British Bristol chassis, both of which were modified and commercialized by that firm.

The floodgates were opened in 1951, when Pininfarina created a new body for the ugly Anglo-American Nash-Healey sports car, being subsequently hired to restyle the domestic Nash line. In fact, series-production Pininfarina Nashes existed only in the firm's press releases: his ideas did not lend themselves wholesale, and only some of them were used. It was, however, good publicity for Nash, and even better publicity for the Italians. Over the next few years they moved in on Europe. Pininfarina signed up with Peugeot in 1954, doing the 403 and 404 sedans. He then lent his talents to the British Motor Corporation, applying his razor-edge shape first to the Austin A40, and then to a rationalized 1.5-litre sedan. Austin got an unexpected bonus out of this deal, since Innocenti of Milan acquired a licence to build A40s in Italy, an exercise unthinkable in the 1930s (even forgetting Mussolini's anti-British sentiments).

By the end of the 1960s, the Pininfarina influence extended as far as Argentina, where he styled the six-cylinder Torino coupé for IKA. Nor was he the only Italian stylist to leave an imprint on foreign makes. Volkswagen's sports coupés and cabriolets (1956 on) were built in series by Karmann of Osnabrück to Ghia designs. Ghia also enjoyed a long association with Chrysler, building a whole generation of dream-car prototypes which would influence the standard product in coming years. Produced in limited series were the Chrysler-based Dual-Ghia sports coupés and convertibles, and some very expensive limousines (90 between 1957 and 1960) on extended Imperial floorpans. Boano had a major hand in Renault's Dauphine (1956). Michelotti of Vignale worked with Standard-Triumph in Britain, starting with a tidy-up of the 1956 Standard Vanguard, and progressing to the Herald-Vitesse family. The "fine Italian hand" would penetrate as far as Japan, where Michelotti refined Hino's version of the small rear-engined Renault into the Contessa series of 1964. He was also responsible for the later Dutch DAFs.

The Pininfarina style in its ultimate form was severe and, by the early sixties, critics were complaining of a new uniformity. After all, the same influence was now detectable in the latest Fiats and their French cousins, the Simcas, as well as in the Peugeot 404 and the Austin/Morris clan. The Austin and Peugeot were especially close in appearance. The trend was nevertheless here to stay, and the seventies would see such developments as a Pininfarina Rolls-Royce and a Bertone Volvo.

Alongside these international relations, Italy continued with Fiat *elaborazioni*, a sure line of business in a market where imports were heavily restricted until 1960, and where—at least in the earlier part of our period—90 % of all new cars came from a single factory. An *elaborazione* was exactly what the word implied: one took a standard Fiat and jazzed it up with chromium strip, a new facia and, in the case of the rear-engined 600 and 850, more doors than Fiat themselves considered suitable. One could, of course, go well beyond the bounds of mere beautification, and some staggering things were done to 600s and 850s by Abarth, for instance. The tiny coupés, with their 90–95 mph (145–

(*Left*) Dyna-Panhard sedan from France, 1954 style—or almost the exact opposite of Dante Giacosa's small-car philosophy at Fiat. Two cylinders and front-wheel drive (where Giacosa settled for an in-line four at the back) add up to carrying six people at 75 mph (120 km/h) on 850 cc, 42 horsepower, and a weight of only 1,568 lb (710 kg). What is more, none of this was won at the price of low gearing (top was 4.71 to 1) or excessive thirst: consumptions of the order of 40 mpg (7 litres/100 km) were possible with give-and-take driving. The key to all this was all-aluminium unitary construction—on Panhards the only steel structural member was the tube supporting the front end. Weaknesses were noise, poor synchromesh, an inefficient petrol heater, and the high cost of the lightweight carcass.

(*Opposite, top*) BMW's determined attempts to challenge Mercedes-Benz in the 1950s were financially disastrous, for all the lovely overhead-valve V-8s that it bred. The sedans used updated 1936 styling and looked bulbous, but Munich's answer to Stuttgart's 300S—this Type 503 cabriolet made from 1956 to 1959—was more attractive. Both rivals had four-speed all-synchromesh transmissions with the column shift beloved of Germans, but the BMW retained a beam rear axle, and played safe with carburettors while Daimler-Benz adopted fuel injection. Hence output (at 140 horsepower from 3.2 litres) stayed lower than that of the 300's in-line overhead-camshaft six. The BMW was, however, cheaper in the home market, and annual sales ran at about the same level.

(*Opposite, bottom*) Peugeot made few mistakes in our period. The stolid 403 would account for over 1,100,000 units beween 1955 and 1967, in a range which also embraced the 403/Sept with the old 203's 1,290-cc unit, a diesel variant, a convertible, a station wagon, and a line of light commercials. If rust took over in the end, the 403 proved very tough indeed, with a win to its credit in the 1956 Australian Ampol Trial, and a good record in the East African Safari—this last destined to be almost the preserve of the model's successor, the 404. Pininfarina styled the older car as well as the 404, but he managed to keep the French look, lost by later models which could easily pass for Fiats or Austins from the same drawing-board.

(*Right*) The spyders created by Pininfarina for Alfa Romeo are familiar. Less usual is the four-seater Giulia GTC (1965), one of the last designs by Carrozzeria Touring of Milan. Only 1,000 were made. The car used the famous 1.6-litre five-bearing twin overhead-camshaft four-cylinder engine, and by this time a five-speed all-synchromesh gearbox with well-chosen ratios and floor change was standard. So were servo-assisted disc brakes on all four wheels. The result was expensive—2,395,000 lire in Italy as against 1,570,000 for a sedan—but pleasing, and tremendous fun to drive.

155 km/h) of top speed, really came under the heading of a separate make—but 850TC versions of the 600, still with the regular body, were bored and stroked out from 633 cc to 847 cc and 80 horsepower (standard engines gave 24.5 hp), with a lowered suspension, stronger clutch, special exhaust system, and radial-ply tyres. In its ultimate form, the 850 ran to a twin overhead-camshaft unit with double the original capacity, a nose radiator worthy of a 1920s fighter aircraft, and a top speed of 132 mph (211 km/h): it could stay level with an E-type Jaguar up to 100 mph (160 km/h).

The next stage was to circumvent the problems of custom bodies, when there was no chassis on which to mount them. One could buy a non-running set of mechanical elements—floorpan, engine, transmission, brakes, and suspension—and build a car around them. This practice was followed by Abarth, Siata, Lombardi, and Moretti among others. Abarth also worked on French Simcas, while a parallel industry was developing in France around Panhards (DB were the principal exponents), Renaults (Alpine) and, from 1967, the Simca-based CG. What emerged could be strange. Siata started our period with a conventional MG look-alike based on the Fiat 1400, and ended their career in 1970 with something externally similar, yet having 850 mechanics at the rear. The open Lombardi, also rear-engined, had Morgan and Lotus overtones, the same firm offering an odd little square-tailed sports coupé. At the other extreme, Ghia's Vanessa was a "shopping coupé" for ladies, complete with built-in parcel trays and a two-pedal transmission.

The Italians worked with new components. In Britain and America, however, the novel glass-fibre techniques were originally devised to furnish fresh, cheap bodies for elderly chassis. Despite Ford's dedicated early-1940s experiments with soya derivatives (never, incidentally, applied to coachwork), glass-fibre bodies were a post-war phenomenon, surfacing quietly in southern California in 1950. Early examples were usually adapted to elderly Ford V-8s, and we shall meet these again when we explore the panorama of the kit-car. The new form of construction, though, entered regular chassis-makers' catalogues for the first time on the 1953 Chevrolet Corvette sports roadster, followed a year later in Britain by Jensen's 541 two-door sedan. The pioneers of glass-fibre unitary construction, as we have seen, were Berkeley (1956) and Lotus (1957).

Glass fibre has much to commend it for small production runs, since tooling is cheaper to balance a higher unit cost. Moulds for complex shapes are cheaper than elaborate machinery, and this method of construction also obviates the need for spot-welding in awkward places. It will stand considerable punishment without deformation and, in the event of an accident, one can cut out the damaged section and "knit" another into place. It can be made fire-resistant, and it may also be self-coloured to cut out multiple-cost spraying, although its great durability in such cases has been somewhat offset by the advent of hard, deep, and durable acrylic celluloses from 1964 onward. Plastic bodies have been used successfully by makers in countries like Turkey and Israel, where runs are unlikely to exceed 4,000 a year and there is no presswork industry.

Against the system is the relatively short life of a mould. A run of several thousand can be the limit, as many small specialists have discovered when taking moulds over from defunct firms. One cannot re-paint a self-coloured body when it eventually starts to discolour: and one of the tougher glass-reinforced materials, Expanded Royalite (used on the original 1966 Cord replicar in America), was reluctant to hold a coat of paint for any length of time. Individual panels are occasionally difficult to align, and on open cars there is the problem of door apertures. On the Lotus Elan (1963), internal framing had to be welded up

and incorporated in the mouldings. Thus, in mainstream car manufacture, the chief use of plastic has been confined to individual mouldings—the roofs of D-series Citroëns, the bonnets of Singer Hunters (1955), and the boot lids of Honda minicars from 1968 onward. The material has, of course, been in wide use for dashboards since the later 1930s.

Not that many manufacturers have not used glass-fibre bodies: there were 19 such users in 1963, and 26 in 1969. What is significant is that few of them were true volume producers, and those who were did not apply the material to their best-selling items. The highest annual production rate recorded—about 30,000 at peak—stands to the credit of the pioneering Chevrolet Corvette, but such an output is a drop in the ocean to a company with a total potential of two million units a year. Of other major makers, Studebaker used glass-fibre on their exciting Avanti coupé (1962), yet were frustrated by failing finance as well as the usual headache of panel-fit. Saab's contribution was the short-lived, low-volume Sonett sports car. As for the rest, they consisted of firms in emergent countries (Anadol in Turkey, Sabra in Israel); Reliant, the British makers of three-wheelers and sports cars; and an assortment of kit-cars and specialist machinery employing British Leyland, Ford, GM, Renault, Rootes, or VW mechanical elements. Most of the latter were British, but there were also manufacturers in the U.S.A., Belgium, Germany, and France, plus a Greek minicar—the Alta—based on the German Fuldamobil.

With the convertible on the decline, a situation had been reached in 1969 when only one major European maker, VW, was still building the style in real quantity. Their plain Karmann-bodied four-seater had always outsold the Karmann-Ghia with its sportier lines. However, some interesting variations were seen. Power tops had long been common in America, although for the less expensive European models this was an unnecessary complication. Austin offered one on their big four-cylinder Atlantic and Hereford types (1949–52), while the later Daimlers and Dagenham Fords had an infuriating system in which the hydraulics were applied only to bring the top into a half-erected position. The four-door convertible was largely dead, Kaiser's version barely lasting into 1951: the only other contenders were the Mercedes-Benz 300, current throughout most of our first decade, and the huge Lincoln of which less than 15,000 were built between 1961 and 1967.

An unusual compromise between the fixed-head coupé and the convertible was tried by Ford of America in 1957. On this steel-roofed five-seater, the entire roof section retracted into the boot. Alas, the loss of luggage space and rear-seat legroom were as nothing beside the 6,000 feet of assorted wiring, ten power relays, ten switches, eight circuit breakers, and seven electric motors required to operate this mechanical marvel. The model was dropped after three seasons, despite respectable sales of 48,000 units. A sadder solution, albeit one to catch on strongly in the 1970s, was Porsche's 911 Targa (1966), a coupé with only the roof section detachable. Storage problems were simplified, while the solid rear quarters not only gave structural stiffness but also served as a crash pylon. In a safety-conscious world, this was a necessary compromise, although it is significant that Porsche returned to real convertibles in 1982!

The station wagon—roomier than a sedan, less discriminatory than a limousine, and adaptable to unitary techniques—went marching on through both our decades. True, it had yet to become a five-door, dual-purpose sedan, but equally it was neither servants' transportation nor the plumber's best friend. Indeed, station wagons embraced a vast range from the stripped *commerciales* of France (seats and not much else) to the luxury nine-seaters of Buick or Oldsmobile. As late as 1970, the most rudimentary class was represented by Britain's Bedford Beagle, a

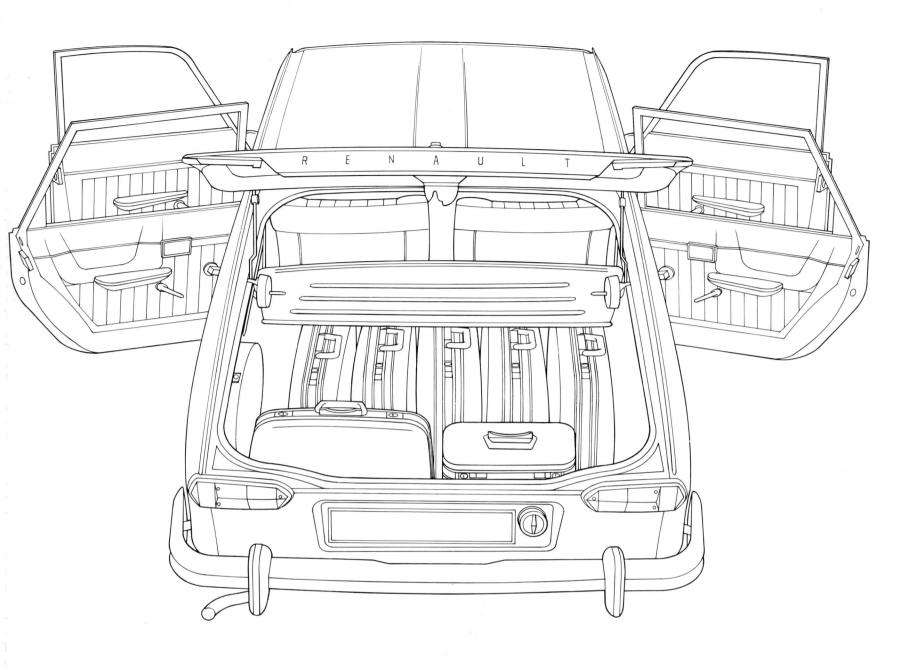

Enter the hatchback, or what can be done with a new style, given the flat floor conferred by front-wheel drive on the 1965 Renault 16 sedan with 1,470 cc. Interior accommodation could be arranged with any combination from free bedroom for two to enough luggage for a sizeable expedition. And even as a four-door family sedan, there was plenty of space, with no access problems for either passengers or their bags. The handy volume at the rear in normal use (*above*) could be doubled by tilting the rear seat forward and suspending its backrest on straps (*below left*). The latter might also be tilted so as to meet the backrest of the front passenger's seat, forming an enormous inclined lounge-chair, until both front seats were arranged flat for sleeping (*below right*). Adjustment was manual by means of locking levers, the seats sliding on ball-bearing runners. Fortunately, a heavy load in the boot did not result in a higher headlamp beam when driving, as a switch was available to lower the beam.

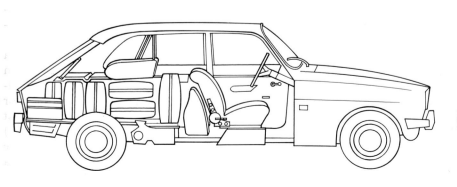

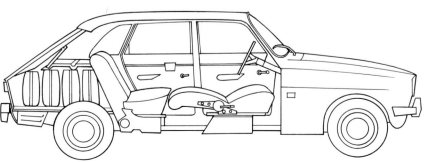

(*Above*) The Great American Norm, or one of 128,582 Chevrolet Bel Air Hardtop Coupés of 1956, a production statistic that would be creditable for any European maker's *whole* range—in Germany only Volkswagen and Opel would surpass it that year. The 4.3-litre V-8 engine was not particularly powerful (165–170 horsepower, or 205 with all performance options), and the base specifications still spelt a six-cylinder unit and three-speed manual. One could, however, "load" one's Chevy with automatic and power steering, brakes, seats, and windows, besides air conditioning and (from this year) seat belts.

(*Opposite, top*) Apart from Mercedes-Benz and a few cars from Kaiser-Frazer, Lincoln was the only firm to market a four-door convertible during our period, whereas in 1938 there was a diversity of offerings from GM, Chrysler, and Ford. Stylistically, the 1961 Lincoln had affinities with the six-passenger Thunderbird, and it was also unitary, but its wheelbase was 10 in (25 cm) longer, while the engine was a huge 7-litre V-8. The power-operated top was a real necessity, as anyone will know who has grappled with the opening and closing of a large British or German formal cabriolet of the 1920s or 1930s.

(*Opposite, bottom*) Colour used to break up slab-sided masses: the poor little Metropolitan 1500 (this is a 1961 model), made by Austin for American Motors, certainly needed it. Comparisons with Neapolitan ice cream were inevitable, but it has never been easy to scale a sixteen-foot (say 4.9-m) sedan down to a mere 149 in (3.8 m) of length. What looked right on a straight-eight in 1933 looked stunted with the shorter bonnet of a six, and the rules hadn't changed. Over 95,000 Americans, however, fell for the little Anglo-American, and it had quite a following in Britain, too.

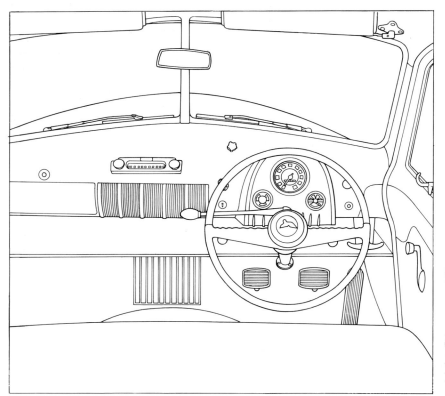

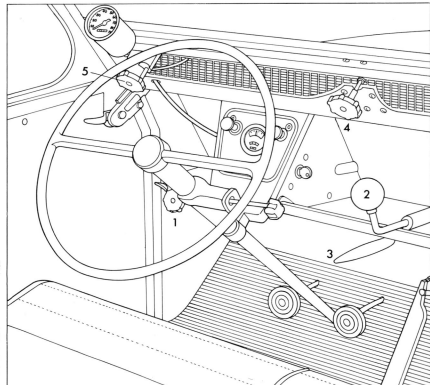

conversion of a light van using the mechanics of the Vauxhall Viva, though not the current styling, the sheet metal being a holdover from 1964. This had seats and windows, but little sound damping, while the combination of the latest engine and high-ratio back axle allied to indifferent drum brakes made it an exciting vehicle to drive in the wet.

The wagon's share of the U.S. market remained steady at about 11% overall, and it became an essential element in makers' programmes elsewhere. Offerings were limited in 1951, coming from Austin, Hillman, and Standard in Britain, Ford and Opel in Germany, Peugeot in France, Fiat in Italy, and Skoda in Czechoslovakia. All were van types except the latter two. In fairness, the French 2CV Citroën, nominally a convertible sedan, counted as a dual-purpose vehicle, but choice was restricted. By 1955, however, there were wagons by such firms as Borgward, DKW, Morris, Renault, Simca, and Volvo, soon to be joined by Citroën, Humber, and Vauxhall. On the other hand, the "woody" was a thing of the past, and extinct in America after 1953. We were also heading away from the van-with-windows school of thought, even if this persisted in Japan right into the late sixties. Bodies were still truckish, rear seats were uncomfortable, and not a few makers considered two doors and a tailgate sufficient.

Gradually, though, the concept of a sedan with an additional tail section began to take over. Rambler led this trend in the U.S.A. in 1957, and more and more refinements followed. Studebaker's 1963 model with sun-roof was not copied, nor was the rearward-facing extra back seat on Saab 95s. But by 1966, American wagons featured tailgates that opened either sideways or downward, and the power-operated type made their appearance a year later. By the end of our period, anyone with the right money could take his pick of a huge range, from the tiny Mini (still with a wood-straked option for the traditionalists) up to the colossal nine-seaters of Ford, Buick, Oldsmobile, and Pontiac, 18 ft (5.5 m) long and good for nearly 125 mph (200 km/h) on 6.5 litres of V-8 with the usual power options.

From this it was only a step to the true "combination car". This label conjured up visions of the *camionettes normandes* (farmer's tourers) offered

by Citroën and others in the twenties. Citroën had in fact revived the theme on their 2CV in 1948, since it featured quick-detachable seating and a canvas one-piece top extending down to floor level at the rear. Thus it could double as a car or delivery van and, with the hood furled, a wardrobe or a grandfather clock could be carried. Sedans with rear tailgates were offered by Chrysler and Kaiser in the early fifties. A one-piece, swing-up tailgate made Citroën's last long-wheelbase *traction* (1953–57) into an old-school *commerciale*, if an unwieldy one. A further advance was the Farina-styled Austin A40 (1959), although in sedan form it was no hatchback, as the rear window was fixed, even if the boot-lid gave access to the rear of the body: only on the later Countryman version did the whole rear panel open. The real breakthrough, however, came with such cars as the Renault 16 (1965) and Austin Maxi (1969), using a true five-door sedan configuration with proper seating. In both these cases, front-wheel drive permitted an unobstructed flat floor at the back. A trend was being started—by 1982, 29 makers in seven European and Asian countries were listing three- and five-door styles as well as (and sometimes instead of) the traditional two- and four-door types.

Chevrolet and Pontiac had already produced sporting two-door wagons in 1955, but these did not catch on, and the true "sports" model arrived only in 1969 with the much-imitated Reliant Scimitar. This part of the story belongs to the seventies. Not that the van-type wagon was finished—it merely assumed a new and more apposite direction. Volkswagen's Transporter (1950) and Fiat's Multipla (1955) exploited rear-engine techniques to the full, with maximum carrying capacity crammed onto the shortest possible wheelbase, and true forward control in the commercial-vehicle sense. In due course, there would be a parallel development of the Chevrolet Corvair: its 1965 replacement, the Chevyvan, would adopt the layout despite a return to a front-mounted, water-cooled engine. While many vehicles in this class were used as station wagons, their main impact, as we shall see, would be in the realm of the mobile home.

Limousines, landaulettes, and sedancas were in decline, largely be-

118

cause the wealthiest motorists tended to opt for up-market editions of regular sedans (Cadillac, Jaguar, Mercedes-Benz) or drive themselves in the new generation of GTs and sports coupés. Of fourteen firms offering assorted formal carriages in 1951, only seven were still quoted in 1960. By 1969, those who preferred not to drive themselves, and also required the snob features of a division and occasional seats, had a simple choice: mainly Cadillac, Daimler, Rolls-Royce, and Mercedes-Benz, not to mention a price tag in excess of £6,000. Of these, the Phantom VI Rolls-Royce was strictly tailor-made, and the 6.3-litre V-8 Grand Mercedes by no means a regular showroom item: only 336 were delivered that year. Daimler's production ran at about 200 units annually, while Cadillac's fluctuated between 1,500 and 2,000 regardless of the *marque*'s overall sales performance. That other specialist vehicle, the up-and-coming 4×4, was not geared to any particular body type, and will be dealt with elsewhere in this book.

Of the accessories, the spare wheel remained a permanent headache. The side-mount had long gone, and external rear stowage was used only on traditional sports cars (pre-1956 MGs, Morgan, Lotus Seven). An odd and persistent hangover was the Continental spare wheel, a strange euphemism for what had, after all, been general practice up to 1934. Its new sobriquet stemmed from the vertical, exposed rear mounting used on that splendid if slightly misguided Classic, the Lincoln Continental of 1940–48. Suddenly in 1952 this became a cult object, and accessory makers started to offer "Continental kits" for almost any American car. Kaiser and Nash standardized it on some

models, the latter's including the curious little Austin-built Metropolitan, while all the big three manufacturers listed installations in their accessory catalogues. The cult spread to Britain, where Dagenham Fords started to sprout such excrescences, albeit not as factory options.

It was all over by 1959, though there were some peculiar side-effects. Lincoln revived the Continental theme in 1956 and, while the spare wheel was no longer outdoors, its presence was commemorated by a moulding in the boot lid. Even worse was Chrysler's "sport deck", a disease either optional or—occasionally—standard on various models of the 1957–61 era. This consisted of the impress of a spare wheel and its cover on the nearly horizontal deck lid, and the resemblance to the top end of a dustbin was only too obvious. Mercifully it died, but the third redesign of Lincoln's two-door Continental coupé (1968) featured a near-surrealist tail bustle, last flowering of a strange fad. Otherwise, spare wheels tended to live in boots, except on rear-engine cars where they helped to limit the space available under the frontal "bonnet". Odd locations were in the front wings (Bristol) and over the engine on such cars with front-wheel drive as the D-series Citroën and the Renault 16: as the former was cramped anyway, not much accessibility was lost, and indeed a little was gained by mounting the tool kit inside the wheel. Honda claimed that their under-bonnet mounting protected the passengers. The older idea of a separate access tray under the boot—usually behind the number plate—was dropped quite early in the 1950s, being prone to rust, although some such systems survived to the end of our period, as did those in which the wheel was mounted

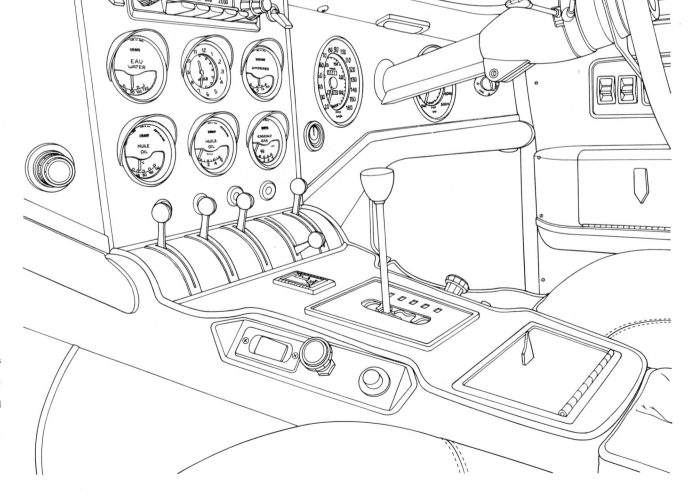

Facias of the fifties, not a good period for instrument displays. Very American was the original 1948–53 Holden from Australia (*opposite, left*) (the absence of a heater is to be expected in a country where snow is virtually unknown) though other influences are detectable in the circular dials. There is precious little on the dash of the 2CV Citroën (*opposite, right*) as originally marketed (this is a 1953 model), which offered only an ammeter and a speedometer, the latter apparently an afterthought. The headlamp tilt control (*1*) was necessary to adjust the lights to the self-levelling suspension. The gearshift (*2*) is the now-traditional Citroën dashboard-mounted type, and the handbrake lever (*3*) lives on the dash as well, like the air control (*4*). Twin wipers (*5*) are provided: they can be worked by hand if the power source fails.

(*Right*) Birth of the console—although this Facel Vega with 6.3-litre Chrysler engine is the 1962 model, rather than the original 1954. The theme is light aeroplane, with speedometer (angled inwards) and rev counter in front of the driver, secondary dials and radio grouped in the middle, and aircraft-type tumbler switches underneath. The floor-mounted automatic gearshift (or the "stick" for the alternative four-speed manual transmission) lives in the centre of the console, with six controls alongside. To the driver's right on this right-hand-drive car are the controls for the electric window lifts. Not all the walnut cabinet-work is, however, of wood.

Styles change, even on Lancias, though differences go far beyond the traditional grille of the 1953 Appia (*above*)—this is a 1957 *berlina*—and the modern Pininfarina shape of the 1960 six-cylinder Flaminia (*left*). Both are unitary, but the Flaminia's basis is a punt-type frame with deep box-section side members. Both retain the narrow-angle vee engines used on all Lancias since 1925. On the Appia, however, the famed sliding-pillar front suspension is retained, whereas the later car features more conventional coils with short and long arms. On a popular 1,100-cc sedan, too, there are attempts to cut costs by dispensing with the complex transaxle and inboard rear brakes of the parallel Aurelia six: a conventionally located four-speed synchromesh gearbox and semi-elliptic springs take their place. Doors lack pillars, while both weight and corrosion are kept at bay by using aluminium for these, the trunk lid and hood. The engine is almost incredibly compact, but the car had to compete against Fiat's *Millecento* in Europe, and it took ten years to sell 100,000 units. The Flaminia came with 2.5-litre or 2.8-litre engine: all but the first few cars had disc brakes as well, but there was little market at that time for big family sedans in Italy, and the big Lancia offered no international competition for Mercedes-Benz, Jaguar, and the even more complicated Citroën. Sales of 3,386 *berline* between 1957 and 1970 told their own story, although the short-chassis sporting Flaminias fared somewhat better.

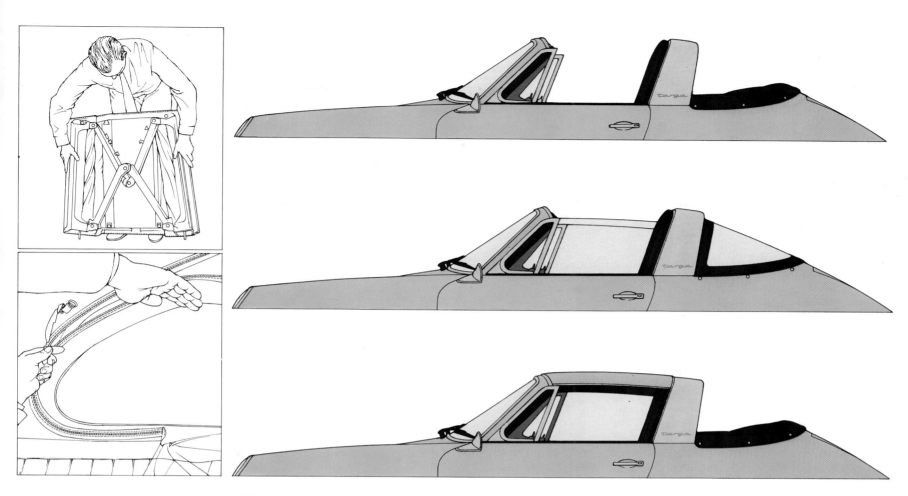

(*Above*) "Four in one", said the 1967 Porsche catalogue of their then-new 911 Targa. Top and rear window were detachable, and the side windows could of course be lowered, giving passengers the choice of fresh air plus safety, sun without draughts, fresh air without rain down one's neck, or sedan protection. The price? Where does one put the detachable bits when one is not using them? The roof folded, to occupy "minimum space" in the front luggage compartment, and the zip-up rear window lived on the parcels shelf. What one did in a sudden shower isn't stated.

(*Right*) Here is how the complete Porsche looked in 1972, by which time the flat-six engine had a capacity of 2.3 litres and was available in various states of tune, with either twin carburettors or fuel injection, and outputs from 130 to 190 brake horsepower.

It's ergonomic if the press department can persuade the customers that it is: some facias of the 1960s. Quite a good luxury sporting example from 1966 is (*left*) the Italo-American Iso Rivolta IR340 coupé with Chevrolet V-8 engine, easily adaptable to left- or right-hand steering. The black-faced dials are well grouped, but there is no clear indication as to the function of the six tumbler switches on the lower middle of the dash (for main lights,

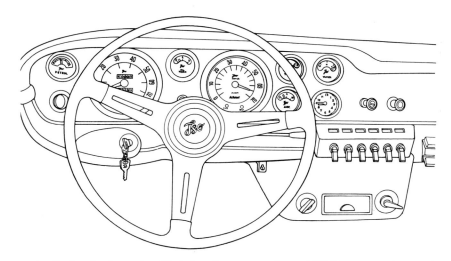

vertically in the boot itself. A less happy notion of GM's was to locate it in a well above floor level at the front of the luggage space, leaving plenty of room for suitcases, but requiring the services of a contortionist to extract the wheel. Fortunately, improved tyre technology meant fewer punctures . . .

In-car living was taken seriously, as Chevrolet's 1953 accessory catalogue shows. Heater/defroster units were still extra, and would not become generally standardized for another ten years. But also available were seat-covers, radio (with or without rear-seat speaker), trunk lamp, screenwash, glare shade, automatic headlight dimmer, electric clock, cigar lighter, tissue dispenser, and plug-in electric shaver. The 1958 list had one serious addition—air conditioning—and one comedy item, the vacuum ashtray ("Cigarettes placed in this tray vanish like magic when the lever is pressed"). Heaters were mainly of fresh-air type, although air-cooled Panhards came with a petrol-fired device of somewhat dubious efficacy.

Real air conditioning—Nash's much-plugged system was merely a form of controlled ventilation and heating—arrived on Packards as far back as 1941. This was revived after the war as an option of 1953 Cadillacs, costing $619 (£221), and the other American makers followed soon afterward. It was taken up in the Old World by Rolls-Royce in 1956, and Jaguar were offering it on their prestige sedans by 1965. In most parts of Europe, however, such a refinement was superfluous, and even in 1969 the option was confined to the more expensive cars, like Ferrari and Mercedes-Benz.

Radio tended to be an extra throughout our period, and stereo—a 1960s phenomenon—even more so. Apart from Rolls-Royce (who invariably fitted a radio as standard) and oddities such as the Russian Volga, a radio was inclusive only when an importer wanted to justify the higher price with superior equipment. The Japanese were especially adept at this: all *de luxe* Toyotas sold in Britain included in-car entertainment. Nonetheless, more and more cars had radios. In 1935 approximately 1.2 million cars were so equipped in the whole of the U.S.A, whereas 7.5 million new models (91% of national production) were sold with radio in 1969. In Britain, however, of 341 cars tested by *Motor* between 1961 and 1967, only 174 offered in-car entertainment, and only 17 of these had it as standard.

Of other amenities, Nash had offered seats convertible into a bed on their 1930s models, and in the 1950s their accessory catalogues included plastic blinds for the rear windows on such occasions. From the early 1960s, reclining back-rests began to catch on, and in the later sixties they would be standardized on a number of the more expensive European cars. In 1950 the screenwash was very much an extra, even though it could be specified as factory equipment. By 1960, its use had become almost universal, and most motorists were wondering how they had managed without it. Refinements of the system included electric operation—a great improvement on the squeegee which could shower water over the driver's knees if pressed too energetically—and an intermittent wash/wipe device which had reached the better middle-class cars by 1966.

Sunroofs were also coming back into prominence by the later sixties, a direct result of the convertible's declining popularity. Originally they had been a British preserve: the only major European firm to adopt them was Peugeot, although General Motors had tried such an option in 1939–40 and found few takers in America. A number of British factories persisted with the theme after the war—but as sliding roofs let in monsoon rain and dust with equal lack of discrimination, Britons bowed to the exigencies of the export drive and went without. Even Rolls-Royce ceased to offer it on their standard bodies after 1955. The Golde canvas-insert type, however, continued to sell well in Germany, while certain standard bodies (Fiat's twin-cylinder 500 of 1957, for instance) were a compromise between the full-length cabrio-limousine and the old-school sunroof type. Volkswagen's adoption of metal sunroofs in 1964 presaged a return to the old idiom in a more reliable, metal-panel form, with or without electric operation. BMW, Ford in Europe, Peugeot, and Renault offered manual versions in 1969: on a Mercedes-Benz, one got power assistance.

Power windows had been a regular option on Cadillacs as early as 1953, and 1957's Mercury Turnpike Cruiser carried matters still further with a power seat incorporating a built-in "memory": once set in the appropriate position, it would slide back when the ignition was switched off, returning to its pre-set point when one restarted. By 1963, most Cadillacs had seats with powered six-way adjustment, while similar types were recognized options on other American cars. On Cadillacs of the later sixties, one could have power assistance for door locks, trunk lids, and ventipanes as well. However, most of these aids were extra,

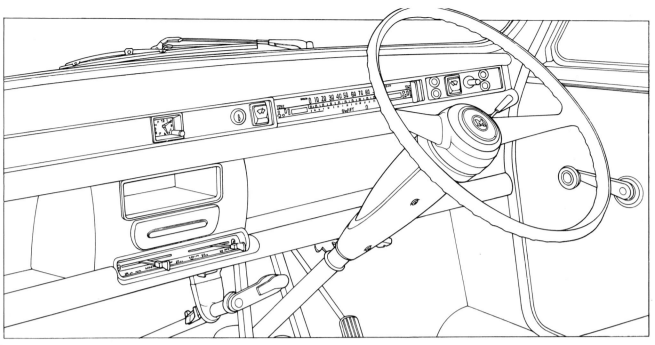

panel light, interior light, heater fan, rear-window demister fan, and fog lamps). As for the dials, the larger ones (for revs and speed) are easier to distinguish than the smaller ones (clock, water temperature, oil temperature and pressure, ammeter, and fuel gauge). The panel itself is crash-padded in anti-dazzle material, as is that of the contemporary BMW 1800Ti (*centre*), on which the gearshift really does "fall conveniently to hand". Typically German is the horn-ring, but wood-graining will be simulated on a relatively inexpensive sedan. There is some bogus wood, too, on the front-wheel-drive Austin/Morris 1800 of 1968 (*right*), with clock, ashtray, and radio space grouped neatly in the centre. Less pleasing are the linear speedometer and that deplorable 1940s hangover, the umbrella-handle handbrake. As these facias show, one advantage of having a simpler car was to remove some distractions from the driver's field of vision.

and in Europe they were reserved for prestige offerings. Power windows, for example, were found on cars such as Iso, Jaguar, and Rolls-Royce. Heated rear windows, those essential adjuncts of 1980s motoring, were regularly available by 1961, but only just beginning to penetrate beyond the executive-car market in 1969 on cars like Rover and BMW. Further, they were still on the extras list. We were a long way from the days when it would be possible to buy a European Ford model inclusive of headlamp wash/wipe, stereo, tinted glass, and power windows.

Wholesale acceptance often breeds a dreary uniformity, but the one place where this never occurred on a motor car was, perhaps, where it was most needed—on the dashboard. There can be nothing so infuriating as minor controls which work in an unexpected manner. True, in the inter-war period there were some oddities, such as the back-to-front gear gate of Vintage Buicks and Dodges and certain 1930s Wolseleys. The French multi-purpose stalk control for lights and other ancillaries was not very common outside that country, and turn-indicators could be maddening afterthoughts on cars from countries where they were not compulsory (they were illegal in some states of Australia, so Holdens dispensed with them altogether). Even starters could be difficult to find, although the "pedomatic" (foot-operated) types beloved of Americans in the thirties were on their way out. Key-starting, a Chrysler innovation of 1949, had attained wide currency by 1961, and was virtually universal six years later. This eliminated some of the less pleasant devices, notably Fiat's plunger-type key, which was pushed in for ignition and rotated for lights!

Facias did, however, move slowly towards the ergonomic. The lunatic rectangular displays of the forties and early fifties, inspired by some weird whim of the stylist, became less frequent by 1960. Prime horrors of the initial years were the strange binnacles of Nash and Panhard, set on the steering column. This meant that the driver had to re-focus his eyes every time he consulted his instruments, not to mention the electrical risks of a profusion of wire extending down the column. Among the few obvious merits of the late-1960s safety legislation was that the demand for collapsible columns led to the removal therefrom of many items which should never have been there in the first place.

After 1959, there was a welcome reversion to circular dials, and from the early 1960s they tended to have black faces. Nonetheless, the linear

speedometer continued to earn its adherents—at the end of our period, it was found on a number of American cars, as well as on models from Leyland, Renault, Simca, and Skoda. It was certainly an improvement on the white-faced, arcuate instruments of certain Rootes cars in the early and middle fifties. Instruments were also uniformly grouped in front of the driver: even the Mini had fallen into line by late 1969.

What went on the panel? Here, two warring factors were at work, the desire for simplicity and the need to furnish information to a more knowledgeable generation of drivers. To some extent, the information required was not the same as in the 1930s, when the dials to watch were the thermometer and the oil-pressure gauge, both potential harbingers of expensive noises. Sealed-for-life cooling systems and stronger crankshafts, however, had changed the situation, and a rev-counter was probably more useful on small units which were safe up to 6,000 rpm. This was certainly necessary on a Wankel, which would give no audible warning of stress when approaching its safe limit. Ammeters, in some form or other, were likewise more important, since the march of the ancillaries was faster than the march of the alternator. Indeed ammeters, thermometers, and oil-pressure gauges continued to be found on the majority of up-market cars throughout the fifties and sixties, with the thermometer as the last to vanish when a maker had to economize. Rev-counters were usually adjuncts of the sports car, although they also appeared on sedans with a "GT" label and featured in the "performance packs" of American makers.

At the bottom end of the market, facias were almost bare. Early VWs offered merely a speedometer, but the 2CV Citroën also had an ammeter and, on the sub-utility antiquated British Ford Popular (1954–59), you got a fuel gauge. Simca's Aronde had an "oil-pressure indicator" (something, it would seem, rather less than a gauge), though it featured warning-lights for low oil pressure, low fuel, and dynamo charge. Early Minis had a single central dial supplemented by warning-lights, and these devices gained in quantity and complexity from the mid-fifties onward. A fairly expensive 1962 model, the Alfa Romeo 2600, had lights for the choke, generator, fuel reserve, ignition, and lamps. Mercedes-Benz and others threw in one for the handbrake: on the Rover 2000, this light also showed if the brake-fluid level fell too low. Perhaps the extreme case of "idiot lights" was found on Fiat's 2300 S coupé (1961), a poor man's Ferrari and an early user of power windows. What drivers

123

Thunderbird development. Here (*opposite, top*) we see the 1956 edition of Ford of America's original two-passenger "personal car" in soft-top guise, with the famed Continental Spare Wheel Kit as standard equipment. Like Chevrolet's Corvette, this was little more than a shortened standard chassis, but creature comforts were more carefully studied, and automatic was not compulsory although power brakes, steering, and top were. The automatic variant set the later fashion for floor-mounted gear selectors. The original 4.8-litre "Thunderbird Special" V-8 was exclusive to this Ford model, but was available in Mercurys—as was the 1956

5.1-litre development, though you could only have this latter with automatic. By 1963 (*opposite, bottom*), the breed had degenerated into just another large American two-door car, available with hard or soft tops, and without any of the elegance of the rival Buick Riviera. An odd variation that year was this Sport Roadster with its wire wheels and racing-car-style headrests. The latter had no more than an add-on glass-fibre "tonneau cover" concealing the rear seats, and most people were disinclined to pay the extra $650 asked. Standard engine in this one was a 6.4-litre, 300-horsepower V-8, and there was no manual transmission option.

(*Below*) You can't call Buick's 1953 Skylark convertible a sports car, for all those genuine wire wheels, the plunging belt-line, and the 188-horsepower edition of the brand-new 5.2-litre V-8 engine with its quadrajet carburation. The car was, however, loaded with equipment usually reserved for the extras

list: power steering, brakes, and radio antenna, besides tinted glass and whitewall tyres. At $5,000, too, it cost nearly twice as much as the regular Roadmaster ragtop with the same engine in detuned form. Sales of this Skylark and the less attractive 1954 version totalled only 2,526 cars.

remembered was, however, a battery of ten warning lights, plus two bells, to signal overheating or an engine speed of over 2,000 rpm with the choke out. It was only a step away from buzzers which sounded when seat belts were unfastened.

Although suction and camshaft-driven systems survived into the 1960s, especially on American cars, the electric screenwiper was standard practice. Twin installations were universal, and triple wipers would arrive with the vast panoramic screens of later mid-engined GTs. Two-speed devices, if not general practice, had reached the upper echelons of the 1.5-litre sedan market by 1969.

Another dilemma, then, was being faced by designers. Idiot lights were confusing enough, but there was also the problem of an increasing number of items which did not properly belong to the conduct of a car—the heater and its fan, the power-window switches (usually on the driver's door), the radio, the cigar lighter and, eventually, the stereo cassette. Standard 1950s practice had been to "style" the radio into the dash, or to park it underneath as a chronic knee-barker.

One of the brighter ideas of our period was to build a console below the main facia, to take this overflow of ancillary devices. Here the pioneer was the French Facel Vega of 1954, with its instrumentation likened to that "of a classy private aeroplane". The large-diameter speedometer and rev-counter sat in front of the driver, leaving the centre clear for the other dials and the radio. On the console itself was a row of aircraft-type switches for heating and ventilation, with the gear lever, ashtray, and controls for lights and washer/wipers. Others followed: in many cases, the "console" served merely as storage space for oddments, although on new models of the sixties (Rover, Triumph) it housed the radio, and the Chevrolet Corvette kept its heater unit and clock there. On medium-sized European Fords of the last years, what

INDEX